The New Encyclopaedia of Float Fishing

The New Encyclopaedia of Float Fishing

Billy Lane & Colin Graham

Line drawings by Jim Randell

PELHAM BOOKS

To the memory of a great angler

First published in Great Britain by
Pelham Books Ltd
27 Wrights Lane, London W8 5TZ
1981
Reprinted 1982, 1984, 1987

ISBN 0 7207 1314 5

Typeset by Cambrian Typesetters, Farnborough
Printed in Great Britain by Hollen Street Press Ltd, Slough, Berkshire
and bound by Butler & Tanner Ltd, Frome, Somerset.

Contents

Preface

This new and completely revised version of what has been one of the most popular angling books of the post war era must now, sadly, be considered the last testament of one of the greatest and most popular anglers of recent times. Billy was already an extremely sick man when he was asked to revise his now famous float fishing encyclopaedia. It was typical of him that despite a long series of serious illnesses which caused him a great deal of pain, he was as keen as any that the project should go ahead. Though I've never been a fatalist I find it quite extraordinary that the last telephone conversation Billy and I had (which dealt with the only passage still subject to revision) should have taken place just two hours before Bill entered hospital for the last time. He died only a few days later. Over the years since the first edition was published, it's clear that Billy's ideas have helped many anglers. I know it was his hope that this updating of thoughts will be similarly helpful. This, of course, is the thing all who met Bill will remember him for most . . . his willingness to help anyone improve their fishing. It only remains for me to say that all the ideas in this book, new and old, are Billy's, my main hope being that they have been presented in a way which will continue to justify the claim so often made for him when he was alive . . . that he was the greatest float angler of them all.

Colin Graham
Sheffield 1980

Introduction

For most coarse fishermen their idea of angling happiness is to sit quietly watching a float. For so many, it seems the ideal way of fishing and the one which brings them most pleasure.

In the late fifties and through the sixties, there was a big swing to the leger, usually allied with several methods of bite indication of which the swing tip remains the best known.

Such was the impact of this trend, many anglers, wrongly in my opinion, began to cast doubts on the efficiency of the float in many waters and conditions. This was a shame because the picture painted was a false one.

Happily, such thinking did not last too long and I think it would be fair to say that not only has it been shown that floats are as good as ever they were in coping with most eventualities, there has never been a time when float fishing has enjoyed more popularity or brought as much success than the present.

I have always had the greatest faith in the float as an approach. I have never wavered in this view. From letters I have received over the years since the first edition of this book appeared, I know many share this view. To them and to those who may, perhaps, be sampling the joys of float fishing for the first time, this book will always be dedicated.

In it I present all the floats I use, floats which, I maintain, allow me to cope with every eventuality.

It has been a difficult job for in recent times new floats, sometimes involving tricky techniques, have joined the ever-growing arsenal of equipment we use these days in the hunt for bigger and better catches.

Zoomers, Sliders, Sticks, Wagglers and Avons . . . these are but a few of the names we have to conjure with nowadays. To some this ever-increasing variety has been something they have been able to take in their stride. But, for many more, the rapid improvement in float techniques has led to frustration and this is something I hope will be cured for you by reading this book.

In its pages you will find floats old and new. The important thing about them is that as far as I am concerned they are sufficient for any angler to fish every kind of water in the country for every sort of fish—big or small.

Every one of them has stood me in good stead in practical angling conditions over years of successful fishing and any float included here has passed this test and is still doing an important job for me.

But before taking you, logically I hope, through the various patterns I use I'd like to set down a few basic thoughts about floats which I think will help the reader understand more easily what follows.

And I would first like to knock a failing I have found in many anglers. They have a pet float. Regardless of where they are or what they are fishing for that's the float that goes on.

What usually happens is that on one particular day they have caught a lot of fish with this float and, by some weird deduction of their own, have gone on to invest it with some kind of magic power seeing it almost as an automatic passport to success. Goodness only knows how many wasted fishing hours this has cost them!

If you have got a pet float complex get it in perspective now. If it's a float that fulfils a particular purpose, still use it for that job and that job alone.

If, like so many floats, it just looks good and is of the type so commonly seen these days which is meant to catch anglers rather than fish, then chuck it away.

For me a float has three specific jobs to do: (1) simply

to register the bite; (2) to help present the bait; (3) to help you keep in full control of your tackle. And those points are given in order of importance.

Looking at them in detail, the float is the only means of getting in contact with the fish when float fishing and, therefore, it must register the bite as perfectly as possible.

To make sure bites come it follows that the bait must be presented as naturally as conditions permit. The right float —correctly shotted—is essential.

Having assured accurate bite detection and proper bait presentation the angler must still be in full control of his tackle and the problem here is usually the weather. Once again it is the float which can solve this problem for you.

All this may seem elementary to more experienced readers but, in fact, it is remarkable how many anglers overlook these basic facts. So remember, the float must be the right one from three points of view and if it doesn't satisfy all these functions a change must be made.

Just as important is the choice of material used for making the float. Two key factors play a part here—sensitivity and buoyancy.

It's all too easy to have a float that is sensitive but, at the same time, too buoyant. To give a simple example, a sensitive float in turbulent water will give too many false bites.

So, in considering materials for making floats, I find it best to look at them from two points of view, the material for making the stem and the material for making the body of the float.

For me, the most used materials for stems these days are, in no special order, cane, wire, certain of the quills (especially peacock quill) and that comparatively recent discovery, sarkandas reed. Which I use very much depends on the type of float to be made.

For bodies, four materials, I suppose, are most often used: balsa, cork, pith and plastic. I reject plastic for while it can be sensitive, it seems to have little buoyancy. Pith is very popular with those who like to make their floats as much as possible from natural materials. Though not absolutely opposed to it, I think it a bit too buoyant.

That leaves balsa and cork. I used to use cork a great deal as anyone who read the earlier editions of this book will know. These days, however, I have found balsa so versatile and easy to work with I use nothing else. This does not mean, however, that I now think cork inferior. If you prefer to use cork, do so, for it still does the job expected of it as well as ever.

There will be anglers who would quarrel with these findings but, as I have tried to emphasise already, this question of choice is an extremely personal thing.

The most important thing is that whatever float you use you really understand why it is doing the job you want it to do. You must know what movements of that float con-stitute a bite—and I am thinking of movements other than the simple submerging of the tip—and why that movement means what it does.

I cannot emphasise this strongly enough. The pet floats I mentioned earlier are often the only ones the anglers who use them understand in their selection. This is why in terms of float fishing technique so many of them are standing still.

In the following chapters I have treated the floats in a logical sequence starting with the simplest float for the simplest conditions and going on from there to the more complex ones.

In following them through I am sure you will notice the very real developments there have been and I think it worth mentioning that many of them would simply not have been possible had it not been for the introduction of mono-filament line. This truly opened new horizons for the experimental float angler.

Being something of a veteran myself now, my experience runs right through from the old silk lines to monofilament and because I fished through this vital time of change, it does, I feel, give me a proper perspective of the way float fishing has developed.

Some of the floats I shall tell you about will be what one

might term 'specialist' types and you may find that well-made versions of these patterns are not all that easy to come by in tackle shops. Don't accept second best or it will only bring you more frustration. Keep looking for good examples or better still, make them yourself. The diagrams and photographs should tell you most of what you need to know.

1 The Crowquill

The development of floats for coarse fishing over the years has probably been one of the most logical in our sport, starting off from simple beginnings, then becoming ever more complex as time went on, with the greatest leaps forward being made after the introduction of monofilament lines.

Being, I hope, a fairly logical sort of chap, I decided that the best way to help you understand the many methods which can be used with floats would be to follow that same logical line of development.

So we'll start with the grand-daddy of all the floats— the Crowquill.

No float is more simple than this one. None more delicate. In ideal conditions on the right sort of water, it's unbeatable, a fact which explains why the Crowquill has probably been used by anglers longer than any other kind of float.

Today, to my amazement, many anglers have discarded the Crowquill in favour of more fashionable newer patterns. Maybe, too, they're not so often seen in shops these days as they were. That's still no reason for not using them for the chance to fish a Crowquill in the right kind of conditions remains one of the most satisfying experiences any angler can have.

It's part, too, of something I have noticed because I am in the tackle trade myself. So many times I watch anglers go for the new and pretty float in preference to something much less glamorous (like the Crowquill) which almost invariably would do a better job. There are more anglers caught by a pretty float than there are fish, I can tell you!

Nevertheless, it's got to be admitted that Crowquills are not as readily available as they were and, later in this chapter, I'll be telling you about a comparatively recent invention of mine which is a good substitute.

In the meantime, let me present the evidence which, I submit, still makes the Crowquill a must in any self-respecting angler's tackle box.

As you will discover there's more than one form of Crowquill float and more than one way of fishing them.

I intend to begin with the simplest form of all used for the simplest purpose, stillwater fishing (see Fig. 1). The advantages of the float should be obvious. It's slim, so slim that it offers little or no resistance to the water or to the fish, despite the fact that it has an extremely buoyant tip.

The rig shown is the way you would set up the quill for fairly close-in fishing in stillwater in ideal conditions. The day you'd use this set-up there would be no surface drag, no strong wind, in fact nothing extreme about the conditions at all. In other words, a dreamy day.

Look first at the way the float—anything between 5 inches and 8 inches long—is fixed to the line. This is the first important thing to get right. The line passes through a valve rubber about an inch from the tip and then down through the eyelet ring. This is the most natural way to fish it, with the thickest part at the top.

The water we are fishing won't be more than 6 feet deep. Above that depth the simple Crowquill would be rejected and a different float needed—a float I shall be describing later.

The biggest shot (A in the diagram) is only 12 inches below the float. It's put there to aid casting—to make sure the terminal tackle enters the water *before* the float—and also to make certain the float cocks as soon as possible to give you the earliest possible indication of a bite.

Shot B in the diagram is always in the same position, and this, too, helps casting. Shot B and shot C, which

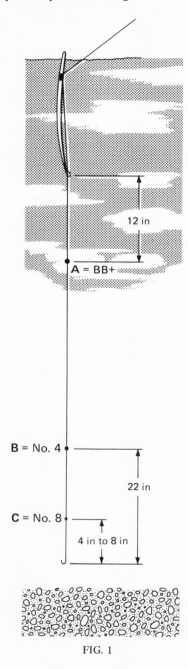

FIG. 1

completes the weighting, also help the natural fall of the bait through the water.

With the shots set like this you get a smooth cast, a trouble-free entry and a natural fall to the bait. Three things happen after entry. Shot A registers on the float first and it sinks a bit. Then shot B weighs in, sinking it a little more. Finally shot C brings the float down until little more than an eighth of an inch of the tip is showing.

It's most important to get used to watching out for these three different registers. Most bites are likely to come after the third register, but you can get them sooner. When this happens the register of shot A or B will be delayed. Strike the moment you notice this! In other words, if the sequence you have come to know is not going according to plan, the assumption, every time, must be that the cause is a fish—a factor worth remembering with most floats.

The emphasis is on shot C as the most decisive one of all. What happens to this shot mostly decides how the bite will be indicated to you. Generally, the fish will swim away with the bait after the tackle has gone through the three settings. In that case the bite will be signalled by the submerging of the float.

If, on the other hand, the fish takes the bait in a way which takes the weight of shot C off the float—by moving up in the water with it—the float will lift to signal the bite. This is particularly true in stillwater, when the fish come up to meet the bait much more often than they would in running water. Look out for those lifts—you're likely to cop for a lot of them!

I hope much of this will have helped to explain the variable measurement of 4 inches to 8 inches of shot C to the hook. This, too, is a vital factor in efficient bite detection.

Let's say small roach are playing with the bait when you have shot C set at 8 inches. The result will be little tips and taps on the float with nothing positive developing. That's the signal to move the shot nearer the hook. It's a question of trial and error. A good yardstick is to always start with shot C 8 inches from the hook and then take action when you've watched developments. Eventually shot C will reach a position when, although you will still get a prelude of tip-taps, there will eventually follow a positive indication.

What I have said so far applies to fishing the bait just off the bottom—as in the diagram. The same rig can be varied slightly to fish on the bottom—laying-on as it's called. Before explaining this I'd like to stress that you'd need even more perfect conditions to do this properly. It follows that if you allow shot C to rest on the bottom you could snag or bury the bait when you want your bait on the bottom, not in it.

The best way to achieve this is to start with shot C 12 inches from the hook. Set the float higher up the line and try a sample cast. If more than an ⅛ inch is showing after the tackle has settled you know shot C must be on the bottom. Move the float back down the line and try again until you have found the critical point at which the tip gives the right amount of 'show', in other words shot C is probably an inch off the bottom while the bait is lying on it.

Before summing up, a word about the size of the float. I mentioned 5 inches to 8 inches. The criteria for deciding which to use is simple—the nearer the bank you are fishing the smaller the float. Don't forget that as you reduce the size of the float the shot, too, must be reduced, although still fixed to the line in the same scale and pattern.

Where would you use this simplest of all Crowquill rigs —and where should you forget about it?

Never use it on water more than 6 feet deep. Never use it in fast running water. Never use it in rough weather. Never use it where long casting is needed.

The right kind of places? Any pond or lake where those conditions are absent. Any normal canal like the Staffordshire, the Lancaster or the Oxford—the small narrow jobs. But there's a rider here. Remember there should be little or no flow. A different setting, as you will see later, is needed when this is the case.

The Crowquill in the form I'm talking about is for sensitive fishing in kind conditions. If you treat it right it will do all you ask of it. Expect too much of it and you'll only meet frustration.

Before I tell you how the simple Crowquill can be used for certain running waters, I'd like to tell you why it has come to gain such an affectionate place in my float wallet and why, over the years, I have come to reject all but one other form of quill float, the exception, as you'll discover later, being peacock quill.

Just as an instance, however, let's take the porcupine quill. I'd never use this in the simple form you see in so many tackle shops. The same goes for goosequills or sea bird quills. I am not against these materials by blind prejudice. I don't want to know about them for a reason which, to me, has become apparent over the years of experience. The great disadvantage of the porcupine—and quills like it—is that its weight in proportion to the shot on the terminal tackle is invariably heavier than with the crowquill. The net result of this discrepancy is that there is a great tendency for the float to overcast with the end tackle finishing up in a tangle behind the float. With the crowquill, the shot invariably precede the float into the water—which is the way it should be.

My objection to porcupine quills rests solely on the way they can interfere with smooth casting. And for me that's reason enough to stay faithful to the crowquill.

Cane has been used as an alternative to crowquill but here again I'm not too keen. This material on its own doesn't give a nice, even sinking action after the float has hit the water. Cane floats often lie flat after the cast and you have to jiggle the line to persuade them to cock . . . a time-wasting procedure which could cost you a missed bite, something I'm always happy to do without!

By now, I hope you have been persuaded about the very real merits of the Crowquill and are ready to hear how this basic float can be used in running water as opposed to still. First I think I had better make it quite clear what I mean by running water in this context. It's no good trying to use the simple Crowquill in heavy or turbulent water. It just won't wear it.

Basically, you need water that is not running too fast and, even more important, is flowing smoothly. There should be no boils or turbulence of any kind in the swim. Weatherwise, the wind should not be strong.

Having found the right swim and the right conditions you should go on to discover that this is where the Crowquill can be used to its greatest advantage. Its perfect slim body enables you to strike at the fish offering less resistance to it than any other float. There's not the slightest danger of the float getting in the way of you and the fish!

The float is fixed to the line the same way—through a valve rubber at the top and down to the terminal tackle via the bottom ring.

It's in the shotting where changes are made. Because of the movement in the water, the shot are put farther down to make the bait sink faster. If you used the same shotting pattern I gave you earlier it's quite likely the bait would pass through your swim without ever reaching the lower depths, where almost invariably you would expect the fish to lie.

To achieve this speedier fall the heaviest shot (A in Fig. 2) is pinched on just 24 inches above the hook—a position which helps it to do its job of getting the bait down without offering any resistance to a taking fish. The dust shot which previously was last on our line has now been eliminated and its place (point B) has been taken by a heavier No. 4 shot.

This is still part of the plan to get the bait down quickly while offering no worries in terms of resistance. The extra weight of this shot is offset by the pull of the water and its real impact on the fish is no more than the dust shot would be in stillwater.

Again a variable measurement—from 4 to 18 inches—is given for this shot and, as in stillwater, the reason is the same: to overcome shy bites. The less distinct they are the nearer shot B should be moved to the hook. Eventually, you'll find the right spot after repeated swims where even shy-biting fish will take the float firmly down below the

FIG. 2

surface. This has an added advantage in running water. Not only does it show firm downward pulls better, it also makes 'lift' bites materialise more.

Bites of this variety are likely to be most common with this setting of the Crowquill when small hook fishing with maggots for roach. Because of the loose feed you are invariably offering, the fish are hovering above the bottom literally waiting for the maggots. When they take the one on the hook they pause for a moment with their fins working like a brake. It's this that gives you the lift bite.

This rig can be varied for laying-on in running water—an alternative I'm inclined to employ a lot more than I would in stillwater. The big difference is that the bottom shot (B) will always be fished on the bottom. For this method it should never be less than 18 inches from the hook.

In addition, you will need to fish over the real depth of the water. How much is something I have a little formula for and this seems to have served me well over the years. Briefly, I fish a foot over the depth for every 4 feet of water. If the swim was 8 feet deep I'd set the float 10 feet from the hook.

With the tackle set like this you'll see that a fair amount of terminal line is actually lying along the bed of the river, including, not too far from the point where the line goes up to shot A, the lower shot B. Should you find that the tackle is not laying-on firmly enough an additional BB shot can be pinched on alongside A. Despite the fact that this should prove too much for the float to carry you will find you are laid on even more firmly with both shot supported. The only proviso—to keep the float steady and prevent it sinking under—is to keep your rod tip in the air with the line running tight to the float, the method many call 'stret-pegging'.

While the rod can be held in the hand to achieve this, I think it's better to support it in a rest, particularly as bites with this rig are so positive it is easy to get hold of the rod in time to hit them cleanly. Without exception a bite will take the float clean under. There are no wobbles or lifts with this method.

For this to succeed it's best if the tackle is thrown downstream and slightly out from the bank and then drawn back to the rod rest. This has the advantage of straightening out the tackle from the rod tip to hook. You might find, especially with the extra BB on, that the float hasn't surfaced. In this case all you need to do is give a little more line from the reel and up the float will come.

I would never, by the way, choose to lay-on in running water from the outset. I always start by swimming the stream and it is only when I feel certain bites are not going to come with this method that I revert to laying-on.

In terms of size I never use the smaller Crowquills for running water. Usually my float will be between 7 and 8 inches long—for swimming the stream or laying-on.

The Crowquill is the float for ideal conditions and, as it is these conditions which most often bring the best catches, that's probably the main reason why it holds such a happy position in the catalogue of floats.

Having said that, don't think we are finished with the Crowquill . . . far from it. So far I've only told you about its simplest uses.

Now earlier in this chapter, I said I would tell you about a float which is a good substitute for the Crowquill. It's an invention of mine I call the Canal Antenna and a float which many now prefer to the Crowquill. The only mistake I made was to use the word Canal in its title for this, I am afraid, has led many to think that it is only for use in canals when, in fact, it is perfect for all still waters. When it comes to the running water conditions described for the Crowquill in Fig. 2, I'd say the Canal Antenna could not compete except where the flow is sluggish and no more than that.

The float has a balsa body and cane antenna, the slim tip offered by the latter being something which offers less resistance to a taking fish. I use these floats in three lengths from tip to ring: 5 inches (capable of carrying two No. 1 shot), 5⅞ inches (taking three No. 1) and 6¾ inches (taking four No. 1). The size to be used depends entirely on the

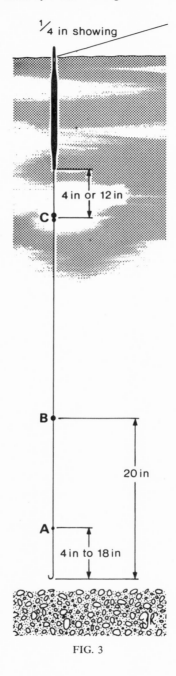

FIG. 3

distance you need to cast, the biggest being capable of being fished four rod lengths out from the bank.

Look now at the diagram (Fig. 3) which shows what I consider the basic pattern for this float. First of all, you can see the float is fixed top and bottom, being secured at the top with a float rubber and, at the bottom, by passing the line through the float ring. This pattern is the one I like to use when fishing with maggot or bread (in the form of paste or punch). Shot A is the tell-tale for bites, this shot being moved nearer the hook the shyer bites are. Shot B is where it is to impart a natural fall to the bait (just like shot B in Fig. 1) while C are bulk shot designed to make the float cock *immediately* it hits the water. You will see I have given a variable distance for their placement. If you are fishing the float top and bottom as shown, these shot should be 4 inches below the float. If, however, there is surface drag or an interfering breeze, you must fish with the float secured *at the bottom only* in which situation you put the bulk 12 inches below the float.

Now before I tell you about other ways in which this shotting can be varied to suit certain baits, let me first have a word about the job of fixing a float bottom only. I have had hundreds of letters from readers of earlier editions of this book expressing puzzlement as to how this is done. Quite correctly, they say that the diagrams suggest that the float is merely threaded through the ring at its base and, that being the case, why doesn't it simply slide down the line to the hook? In other words, how do you keep it in position? The answer lies in the way you thread it. In describing this process again here, I'd like you to bear it in mind all the way through this book whenever you see a float fixed bottom only in this way that this is how it's done. The line is threaded two or three times through the ring but you must be careful. Pass the end of the line through the ring twice. Hold the loop formed tight against the ring then pass the end of the line through again to form another loop being careful when this loop also tightens against the ring that it does not lie over the first loop. Now make a third and fourth loop, again being careful that it does not lie on top of either of the previous loops and making certain throughout that the line never passes between the ring and one of the previous turns.

Now hold the end of the line and let the float dangle. The loops will be reasonably slack and certainly slack enough to let you slide the float up to the position required in relation to the depth of water being fished. Now tighten the loops and the float will remain in position. But what, you will ask, if I want to move the float because I find I have set it at the wrong depth? Rub a finger across the loops and this should loosen them sufficiently to enable you to move the float to its new position. What if it won't move? That will happen if you didn't take care to see that none of the loops fell on top of the other as mentioned above. If the float *is* stuck, you'll have to start again but, believe me, once you have got it right a few times you'll find it simplicity itself.

Let me go back now to alternative shotting for the Canal Antenna when baits other than those already discussed are being used. If you are fishing caster, give the bait a really slow drop. To achieve this, put a single dust shot 24 inches from the hook and then pinch on all the rest of the shot needed to cock the float immediately below the float ring. If you want to fish the increasingly fashionable bloodworm, bulk *all* the shot needed to cock the float between 4 and 12 inches above the hook. Exactly where depends on the strength of bites. The shyer they are the nearer the shots should be placed to the hook. This pattern should *not* be used with any bait other than bloodworm. Experienced anglers will, I'm sure, realise that this pattern merely emulates the teaching of the famous Continental pole anglers who, based on years of success, have found that this is the best way to fish this bait.

To sum up now on the Crowquill and its alternative, the Canal Antenna, let me say this. You are using delicate tackle which means that you should never try to make it fish beyond its limits, especially in terms of distance. That way you will offend against one of the most vital needs set out in my introduction, control. You may face this situation for a number of reasons but, most often, it will be because the wind or the flow have become too strong. That means that you will have to think about changing to one of the other floats mentioned in this book.

2 The Reverse Crowquill—
Darts—Onions

Having spent a chapter indoctrinating you into the idea of the Crowquill, I am now going to turn those thoughts upside down. But don't worry. It's all in the good cause of catching fish. I am talking now about the Reverse Crowquill, a variant of the simple float I've just discussed which helps us achieve more with this material.

As its name suggests, this float is made so that the quill fishes upside down with the ring at the thick end and the tip at the thin one.

It has two main advantages over the simple Crowquill. It will carry a little more lead and therefore extend the limit of your casting distance. And with such a fine tip the resistance of the float to a surface wind is considerably reduced.

From this it should be obvious you can fish with it in rougher conditions than you can with the simple Crowquill. The one disadvantage is that it can only be used in still water. That's because it is literally so sensitive that it's constantly going under in running water, giving you more false bites than true ones.

Let's give an example of when to use it. You are on a lake using a simple Crowquill when a wind springs up. Suddenly you find your casting distance reduced. There's too much ripple. Worse still, the surface drag is going one way, the undertow the opposite way.

All these things can be overcome by the reverse float, in a way which should allow you to continue casting to the same baited areas.

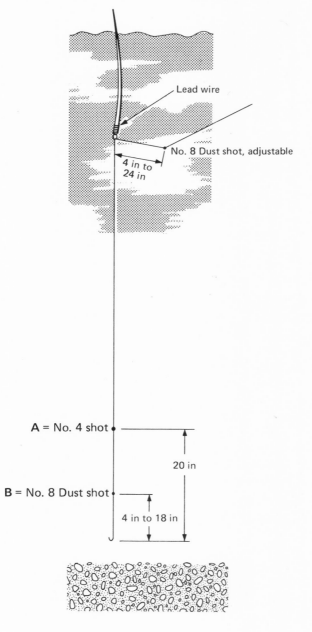

Lead wire

No. 8 Dust shot, adjustable

4 in to 24 in

A = No. 4 shot

20 in

B = No. 8 Dust shot

4 in to 18 in

FIG. 4

For, unlike the simple version, the reverse quill buries your line under the surface. A quick glance at the diagram (Fig. 4) should make this clear. Just exactly how it works is something I'll be telling you in a moment. It's enough to say at this stage that this sinking of the line is often one of the most important factors of all in float-fishing and one you'll find me referring to again and again.

Once more, there's a limit to the depth of water in which to use this float. I'd put it at no more than 5 feet. Above that I think you'll find the float too light to carry the amount of lead you'd need.

The float depicted in the diagram is about 7 inches long and is the only size of Reverse Crowquill I use. Correctly weighted it shows 1 inch at the tip—and the set-up is so finely balanced that the addition of one tiny dust shot would be sufficient to submerge it completely.

The efficiency of this float varies according to the bait. It's at its best with maggots or with bread and other cereals but not nearly so effective with worm, when the weight of the bait can upset the finely calculated shotting.

All floats used to bury the line and beat the wind are fished from the bottom. In this instance part of the plan involves lead wire which you can see wrapped round the float just above the end ring. The lead wire should be fine —but not so fine it will become unwound with use.

Getting this exactly right is essential—and best done before you go fishing. Here's how to do it. Pass a loop of nylon through the float ring and pinch on the total number of shot shown in the diagram—one No. 4 and two dust. Put the float in a bath or tub of water with the loop suspended and then add lead wire until the tip of the float is showing 1¼ inches. I know I said earlier that the float, when fishing, would show 1 inch. It will. That extra ¼ inch in the bath is to allow for the weight of your line when fishing.

When you've completed this test keep the loop of shot with the float in your wallet—then you'll know beyond doubt that everything is going to be exactly balanced when you go to fish.

An odd thing is the number of anglers I've seen using this float fixed top and bottom. They must be crazy for they are defeating all the objects it was intended to achieve.

First, their line isn't buried. Second, the resistance of a reverse quill on the strike is increased enormously. In fact, you are hitting the float first and *not* the fish. With the bottom ring attachment the float collapses smoothly out of the way on the strike and you are straight into the fish.

The shotting—with one exception—is similar to that for orthodox Crowquill fishing (Fig. 4 again). Any bulk shotting up the line has been eliminated by the use of lead wire which has made the float semi self-cocking. Shot A is positioned there to complete the vertical setting and to carry the bait down to the fish reasonably quickly. Dust shot B is our tell-tale for bites and should be set within the limits given according to the strength of the bites. The shyer they are the nearer it is moved to the hook.

The exception is the second dust shot between the float and the rod tip. Its sole purpose is to enable the line to be buried quickly, defeating the wind's pull on the surface and the drag underneath. To gain the greatest efficiency from this shot the rod tip should be kept just under or very near the surface after casting.

Where you place this shot depends on the distance you are fishing from the bank and the speed at which you want to sink the line. The farther the cast the farther this shot should be from the float.

At its nearest setting, 4 inches from the float, you would be fishing not more than one rod length out. This shot has another advantage, particularly when set at the maximum 24 inches from the float ring. It enables you to move the bait slowly and naturally through the water with the minimum disturbance of the tackle. All you have to do is to give a twitch on the line with your reel.

The setting in the diagram is for fishing off the bottom. To lay-on with the Reverse Crowquill it's necessary to make alterations in the shotting. Shot B for this technique should certainly be no less than 18 inches from the hook and there's nothing to stop you making it much more. The main thing to remember is that shot A and the float must be moved up the line the same distance.

You can tell you have got it right because the float will sit a little higher in the water after the cast, returning to its normal 'show' of 1 inch when shot B has reached the bottom. But, as I've said before, I have reservations about fishing in still water with the lower shot on the bottom because of weeds and things. So, mostly, I fish with it just off the bed—in which case the 'show' on the float will be normal.

Used properly the Reverse Crowquill is a handy gadget to have. But like all Crowquills, it must be treated with respect and too much must never be asked of it.

For ponds and lakes in reasonable conditions it's just the job. In canals more care must be taken. The water should be still or moving only at the most sluggish rate. With any appreciable flow at all, forget it.

Now while the Reverse Crowquill is, like the basic Crowquill, not used nearly so much as it was a decade ago, it still has loyal fans and, without any doubt, it performs its task as efficiently as ever. Latterly, however, I find myself preferring a newer type of float. The float—aptly named —is called the Dart and it is a most useful addition to the floats we use for still waters and, especially, canals, in particular as an efficient alternative to the Reverse Crowquill with the added merit that it is easier to use.

The Dart, as I see it, is even more acceptable, however, because it does everything the Reverse Crowquill will do and more. It's more sensitive. It's easier to shot up (the Reverse Crowquill, remember, required fiddling about with lead wire). Because it's straight, it eliminates the 'lean' there was with the Crowquill and, finally, it casts easier.

Look now at our diagrams (Figs. 5 and 6) of the Dart which is a semi self-cocking float made that way by the introduction of just the right amount of loading in the stem needed to make it sit in the water correctly. The stem (which also gives the float that short antenna you can see)

Colour tip
only showing

6 in to 18 in

A   C

B

6 in to 18 in

FIG. 5

FIG. 6

is ¹⁄₁₆ inch diameter cane which is fitted into a slender balsa body which has parallel sides and is loaded at the lower end with a short piece of brass rod to which the ring is whipped.

Like the Reverse Crowquill, the Dart is fished loose with the line passing through the end ring only, thus giving one exactly the same facility for burying the line under the surface when it is windy.

Darts come in three different lengths each having five different loadings, i.e. they carry exactly one, two, three, four or five dust shots, a statement which should immediately impress on you that the Dart works to very fine limits in terms of sensitivity.

To give credit where it is due, the Dart was inspired, to the best of my knowledge, by a type of float devised by Lancashire anglers for bloodworm fishing and, in particular, by that group who were some of the best-known British exponents of this style, those lads from Wigan who called themselves 'The Firm'.

They were particularly successful in a number of matches on the Leamington and Warrington canals and Coventry anglers who watched them were deeply impressed with the obvious sensitivity of the floats they were using. At the same time they reckoned that, if developed, the floats could have wider applications than being used solely for bloodworms. While still retaining the original line and, with it, the float's sensitivity, there was no reason why the float should not be scaled up to enable its use for maggots, caster and that other favourite canal bait, punched bread, and then fished over fair distances.

The original idea then was The Firm's and they deserve all the credit for the basic pattern. Others have now developed it further into the shape in which I am now suggesting you should try it.

The Dart, as its name suggests, is fine on the cast going straight through the air like an arrow, due, mainly, to the loading in the stem.

So far so good. But the next most important, and obvious,

question is when to use which size, especially as the choice seems so wide. Several factors play a part.

The first—and, you might think, the most obvious—is distance. But funnily enough such is the streamlined design of these floats all three sizes are just as capable of the maximum amount of travel any canal angler could want. And almost the same goes for still waters.

The real reason then for three sizes is, in fact, the degree of line sinking one wants to achieve between rod tip and float. The more you want to bury that line because of wind the longer the Dart you select.

In this respect depth also plays a part. The longest of the three floats is 7 inches and obviously you wouldn't want to use one this long in a canal which was only 2 or 3 feet deep. In such a situation you would obviously opt for the smaller length.

Now, as I mentioned earlier, each of these three sizes offers five loadings in terms of dust shots making for a total range of fifteen floats. I think—though others disagree with me—that this is too many for I find it difficult to imagine any circumstances except one of utter desperation when I would feel inclined to use a one dust shot version.

In such an instance, the water would be gin clear and I would be after fishing an extremely slow falling bait in conditions which would have to be absolutely perfect, demonstration enough, I feel, of the limitations of the lightest loading with this float.

Personally, I prefer to work only with those Darts which carry from three dust shots up, and the reason is this. I want a bit of leeway when it comes to burying that line, the sort which will permit me to put a back shot my side of the float to help that line burying process. The float that carries only one or even two dust shots cramps my style extremely if I want to do this. But with three—or more—dust shots to permutate, it can be easily done.

Darts, despite their light loading, permit you to cast with greater freedom. You can put more thump into it compared with other canal floats and particularly, it must be admitted, when compared with the Reverse Crowquill. The latter was best cast underhand or tangles were often the result. The Dart can be cast as you like—underhand, overhead, sideways—in complete safety.

There remains the question of placement of the shot. In normal conditions, with little wind or flow, our first diagram (Fig. 5) is the one which gives you our pattern. Shot B, your tell-tale, moves nearest the hook when bites are shyest. Shot A, to give stability, goes directly under the float. The further back shot C is fixed from the float the stronger the drag.

If it's breezy our second diagram (Fig. 6) gives you the changes. Shot A drops to a position 6 inches above the tell-tale to help guard against tangles while the back shot C is always at 12 inches from the float. The tell-tale B finds its place as before. Now obviously both these diagrams cover only the three dust shot pattern. What happens when four or five are used? The answer is simply that all the extra shot are added at position A in both cases.

For laying-on, adjust the tackle so that there is an 18 inch terminal tail below shot B, the shot itself being just *off* the bottom.

That, then, is the Dart. In my opinion, an improvement on the Reverse Crowquill but one which does not mean the reverse float is no longer of use.

From an alternative to a Crowquill, the Dart, back now to another form of the quill itself.

'Know your onions' is a favourite expression among anglers in the Midlands and when they say it they are not talking about something to eat!

They are referring to yet another version of the Crowquill known, simply, as the Onion.

Looking at the diagram (Fig. 7) you can see the resemblance. If you've not encountered this float before I hope you'll discover, as I did, just what a useful addition to your tackle box an Onion can be, even allowing for the later development of the Dart.

In fact, it is our old friend, the Reverse Crowquill, with

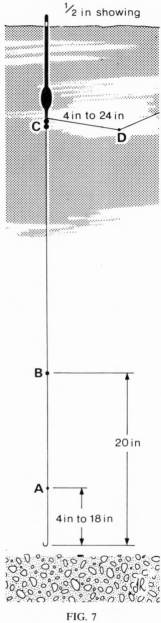

FIG. 7

the all-important addition of a small cork body at the lower end of the float. In shape, this float also gives our first glance at what might be called the earliest form of Waggler float, of which more later.

Its main advantage is that it gives us extra facilities— particularly for casting—that the ordinary and simple reversed Crowquills don't.

The extra 'body' enables you to use more lead, increasing casting distance and giving greater control while basically retaining the sensitivity which is such a feature of Crowquill fishing.

That increased tackle control is particularly noticeable when fishing deeper sluggish water. And remember none of the quills we have discussed so far are suitable for water in excess of 5 feet. With the Onion our maximum depth is increased to 8 feet.

Basically, I suppose, the other Crowquills are for small still waters, mostly when conditions are ideal. With the Onion we are gradually moving into the family of floats which will cope with bigger waters and rougher conditions. The Onion won't cope with the biggest river but there are plenty where it will work a treat. One that comes quickly to mind is the Nene in the reaches above Peterborough. It has served me well there.

The Reverse Crowquill is no more sensitive than the Onion but, to coin a phrase, it's a close-quarters float. The Onion gives us much greater casting distance and can be used in water with a certain amount of flow.

One of the first things you'll find about the Onion is that a lift bite with it becomes a real cracker. No other float I know gives a more positive lift reaction. The tip fairly looms up out of the water in a way which makes the bite absolutely unmistakable—and, of course, that much easier to hit.

Another thing which at first surprised me about the Onion is that, despite its shape, you get little drag or wind resistance. In fact its abilities in this direction are perhaps better than the ordinary reversed quill.

Once again, you will see (Fig. 7) that the float is fished from the bottom but the method used for shotting it has been much simplified since that shown in earlier editions of this book thanks to an improved design which has enabled us to dispense with the fiddling use of lead wire as a balancing agent at the foot of the float. Today, float makers (including myself) take care of this by giving each float a loading in the base of the stem, usually of brass. Another change has been that instead of cork, balsa is used for the body and peacock quill for the stem. The new shotting pattern (Fig. 7 again) is very similar to that shown for the Dart. Indeed, you could argue that it is simply a scaling up the Dart pattern and you would be right. Shot A is the usual tell-tale for bites, being moved, as I've said earlier, depending on the strength of the bites. Shot B helps to prevent back tangles on the cast. Shot C is stabilising bulk which ensures that the float cocks as quickly as possible while D is to beat surface drag, its distance, as with the Dart, varying according to the strength of the drag.

Once more the diagram shows the bait being fished off the bottom and this—almost without exception—is the way I use it. You can try laying-on with an Onion but I wouldn't recommend it, especially when there's even the slightest pull on the water. In these circumstances, it becomes a real jumping Onion, pulling under constantly in a way which makes it impossible to tell clearly whether you've got a bite or not.

Another thing which is different about the Onion compared with the simple reverse quill is the reason governing the distance of the dust shot D which lies between float and rod tip. The distance you are casting is no longer the deciding factor. The thing that counts now is the amount of wind you have to cope with. The stronger the wind the farther the shot is placed from the float ring, although never more than the maximum given in the diagram of 24 inches. The closest setting, 4 inches, would be justified only in the most gentle breeze.

The Onion has one other attribute although it's not one I

often use. It can be set to fish as shallow as 2 feet and yet be cast a fair distance without tangles developing. Anyone who has ever fished this way—shallow and far off—must have found that their end-tackle was prone to tangles in flight. The bulge on the Onion holds the float back in the air without impeding the progress of the leads—and so those tangles are eliminated.

To give you an example, picture a canal where you want to fish under the opposite bank where the water is shallow. The Onion is just the ticket. Quite apart from giving you freedom from tangles, it is just as efficient a bite indicator as ever.

But the Onion does have its restrictions and it would be wrong of me to seem too confident about the variety of its uses. Apart from the restrictions on depth, it should never be used in streamy or turbulent water.

It's fine in all still waters, good in canals and in sluggish rivers. I've already mentioned the Middle Nene and another good example would be for reasonably close-in fishing in the Lower Welland.

In asking you to master all the floats discussed so far, you will soon come to understand *why* you are selecting a certain float for a particular job. That way, you will be able to understand more easily some of the complex ideas which are to follow. Before we progress, however, I'd like to touch on a practical aspect of float fishing for it has a bearing on all the floats you'll find in this book which are fixed to the line by the bottom ring only, what many anglers call a loose float.

I am prompted in this by the consideration we have just been giving to the Onion for this float is, in many ways, typical of this type.

The Onion and the float we discussed immediately before it, the Dart, are the first floats in this book which are described as loaded, i.e. they have weight added at the base of their stems in the making. The reasoning behind this is to permit the float to be cast the greatest possible distance while, at the same time, allowing the shot loading below to be as light as possible. But one of the problems with loaded floats (and if you are sharp you will have picked up the clue to this in Fig. 6) is that when it's windy, and especially when the wind is a facer, there is a greater tendency for back tangles to develop. By back tangles, I mean that the length of line between the float and hook lashes back and wraps round on the cast behind the float. When faced with this situation, and we all are, the answer, as can be seen in Fig. 6, is to move the bulk shot down the line nearer the lower tell-tale shot. In the case of the Onion (Fig. 7), this means that shot B moves closer to shot A, sometimes, in extreme cases, until the two are pinched on side by side. Do remember this tip at all times when you are loose float fishing and I'm sure you will find it invaluable.

Still on the subject of wind, always one of the most important factors affecting the float angler, I have never ceased to be amazed at the number of anglers who fish on blissfully aware, in the loose float situation, that instead of permitting it to be a constant hindrance, they can use it to their advantage.

Think first about the nature of a loaded float. Because of the weight built into it, its path through the air, base first, is bound to be much more direct than if it was not weighted in this way. In these circumstances, the float will invariably be ahead of the end tackle during the cast, this being especially true of floats like the Onion when the weight beneath the float is light. Add now the effect of the wind and it's obvious there will be a still greater tendency for the end tackle to hang back and, in doing so, to tangle round the line. By using the wind correctly and by making use of the tip I have just given about the placement of the bulk shot, such troubles need never happen.

So what do you do? Consider now Fig. 8. What it tells you is that, to be safe, you must cast into the wind and not with it. This means that in the situation shown in the diagram in which the wind is blowing from right to left, the angler must cast to his right—into the wind. The float, as expected, has preceded the end tackle on its flight but

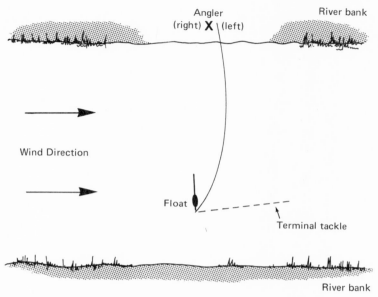

FIG. 8

the latter, because of the wind direction, has been held away (and out of trouble) by the very wind that might have been the cause of the problem. Look at the diagram again now and ask yourself what would have happened if, with the wind in the direction shown, you had cast from right to left or straight to your front and I am sure you will understand that the chances of a back tangle are immediately increased.

If the wind was blowing in the opposite way, i.e. from left to right, then, of course, you would cast from the right to achieve the correct flight shown in Fig. 8.

What, I am sure you will now ask, should one do if the wind is not blowing from one side or the other but is coming from behind or from the front?

It's a good question and the answer is this. In either direction on still water, I say cast to your front. On a river, where flow is an additional consideration, you must think twice. The answer with the wind front or back and with the river flowing from left to right is to make your cast in

41

an upstream direction. If the flow is in the opposite direction then the cast is a downstream one. The main reason for this different approach on a river is not just to beat the wind. If with the river flowing from left to right, you made a downstream cast you would find you had created a big bow in the line between your rod tip and the float. As the need is always to fish as tight a line as possible between you and your float, you would have to make an extra movement of the rod to get things properly tight and, in doing so, would undoubtedly disturb the bait and interfere with its correct presentation. With the correct cast, the line can be tightened comfortably with no effect on the bait. I shall have much more to say about river float fishing in later chapters. In the meantime, if you absorb the tips I have just given you can consider yourself rid of a great deal of frustration in your float fishing.

3 The Zoomer, the Mini-Missile and the Missile

So far, I have told you about floats which will deal with still and sluggish water situations at close to medium range. In this chapter, we move into the more interesting problems of float fishing at long range in this kind of water.

The Zoomer, the first of the floats mentioned in our chapter heading, appeared in earlier editions of this book. I had reservations about its usefulness then. I have even more now. Nevertheless, because of its once great popularity and because, in fairness, it has an honourable place in the history of float fishing, I want to refer to it again for it does give a perspective on what is to follow even though it's no longer getting the headlines it made in the days when it was first introduced. To find out why, let's look first at its development and the reason for it—the need to fish shallow water up to 6 feet in depth at long range.

It was on the lower Welland, a typical sluggish Fenland water in Lincolnshire, where the Zoomer first came into its own and indeed this water is the perfect definition of the type which calls for the use of these floats.

It's not deep—about 7 feet at most. But there is generally a need to cast a bait a long distance while retaining the utmost sensitivity in the tackle below the float.

To the best of my knowledge, the Zoomer was conceived by anglers from Leicester and it was they who made the impact with it in the Welland which led to those headlines I mentioned earlier.

To me, at the time it seemed a logical development from the big cork and quill Duckers with which our Coventry team had then so recently scored in the 1956 Witham National. Whether this was how it looked to the Leicester lads I don't know.

But what is certain is that the Zoomer had all, and perhaps more, of the long-distance casting advantages of the big Ducker without the need to carry so much lead below the float.

In the first Zoomers, this was achieved by carefully moulding lead in a way which retained a streamline shape for the body, giving it the action of a dart on the cast. The stem or antenna was of cane and the ring at the base was supported on a piece of brass rod inserted into the lead body. These early Zoomers had a distinct tendency to waver in flight, a characterisitic which often interfered with casting accuracy. I got rid of this disadvantage by changing the make-up of my Zoomers. I lengthened the stem, using sarkandas reed instead of cane, and reduced the size of the body, now made of balsa, to make it more streamlined. All the weight needed in the body to give it its zoom was in the form of brass rod mounted into the body, this again offering a useful support for the float ring.

The trouble with the Zoomer, and this will seem odd in a sensitive thing like a float, was that it was (and still is) too sensitive. Because of the way it's made and the light shotting it is meant to carry, it will submerge at the slightest disturbance from wind or current, the latter being especially likely on a typically sluggish water like the Welland.

From this, it follows that the Zoomer is extremely prone to go under when the cause is anything but a bite which means that, over and over again, you find yourself striking at nothing with wasted casts the result.

Because of these disadvantages, it is my view that the Zoomer has more than outlived its usefulness though it would be possible to justify its use in one circumstance, when the fish at range in shallow water are also proving extremely shy biters. This circumstance can be dealt with

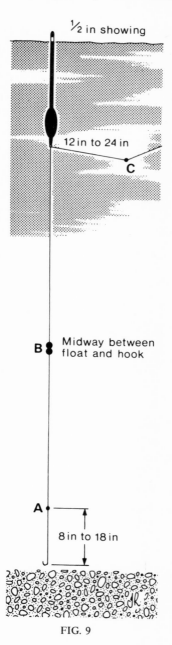

FIG. 9

45

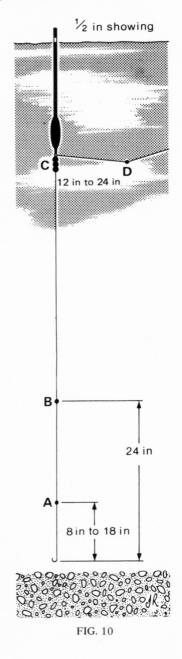

½ in showing

C

D

12 in to 24 in

B

24 in

A

8 in to 18 in

FIG. 10

in other ways but for those who wish to persevere with the Zoomer, the shotting diagram (Fig. 9) shows how. It is a classic light, loose float pattern. The tell-tale (shot A) varies in position for the usual reasons. The bulk shot (B) are placed midway between A and the base of the float. Shot C is the back shot which, hopefully, beats any drag, its placing being furthest from the float when the drag is strongest. The bait should never be fished on the bottom, what is called the laid-on position, for, due to that very sensitivity we have just been discussing, the float will be constantly pulled under by anything but fish. No, with this float, the bait must be just off bottom or still higher in the water. Two variations are possible. If the wind is strong, the bulk shot (B) may be moved, as described for the Onion, nearer A to beat back tangles. The second alternative is when a slow fall is required for a bait like caster. To achieve this, place all the bulk shot (B again) immediately under the base of the float, this approach being known as fishing on the drop.

Now all I have said so far refers to Zoomers when used on rivers like the Welland or on still waters, especially gravel pits. For canal work, however, a much smaller float of the same design should be used and, indeed, the type usually selected is now known as a Canal Zoomer. The type I use is about 6 inches long carrying just two No. 6 shot. It would be fair to describe it as a scaled up Dart. The shot loading is distributed as follows. A dust shot goes on at point A (see Fig. 9 again), a No. 6 at B and a second dust at C. This allows you, for instance, to fish the far bank of a canal with what is an extremely light shot load though, again, I must emphasise that conditions need to be perfect. This small Zoomer, too, can be shotted to fish on the drop. All you do is put shot B directly under the float.

This Canal Zoomer is the only example I still use myself and even that is extremely restricted in view of the need for that rarity, perfect conditions.

As I hinted earlier, however, I wouldn't worry if you haven't got any Zoomers at all. Indeed, I would urge any reader, especially a beginner, to ignore them completely for the float I am going to describe next offers all the advantages claimed for the Zoomer and more, the Mini-Missile. If you were to choose to argue with me and suggest that the Mini-Missile was merely a beefed-up Zoomer, I would have to agree with you though the way I came to design it was not via the Zoomer. It does, in fact, stem from the Missile (a float described in earlier editions of this book and which re-appears later in this one) and as an alternative to the Ducker, a float used for fishing rivers in downstream winds which, as you will discover, has, for me been largely replaced by the Mini-Missile.

You could also say that it was due to thinking big about the Zoomer that this pattern emerged, the final outcome being, however, that I now find myself with a greater selection of Missiles which, in turn, offer more versatility for the float angler.

The scale of that versatility will only become clear when you have read the whole of this book. In the meantime, let's concentrate on the Mini-Missile, a title which suggests, rightly, that these are the smallest of their kind.

They are made of the same materials as the Zoomer, the difference being that the peacock quill stem is longer, the balsa body larger (though still streamlined), and the brass rod loading heavier, the buoyancy of peacock quill as a material playing an especially important role in the effectiveness of this float.

The float will cover you for the same shallow water as the Zoomer but will also fish well in depths up to 8 feet and at a range of up to 40 yards. I carry four sizes of these floats. The smallest is 6 inches long from tip to base, will carry two BB shot and can be cast up to 15 yards. The 7 inch float (taking three BB) will go 20 yards, the 8 inch (two AAA) going 30 yards and the biggest, at 9 inches (taking three AAA), 40 yards.

Look at the shotting pattern (Fig. 10) for the Mini-Missile and you would be right if you described it as a scaled-up version of that for the Dart. Shot A is the tell-tale for bites.

Shot B is the safety first shot to prevent back tangles while C (the bulk) is where it is to give added stability to the float and fast cocking. D is the back shot which beats drag, its distance from the float being greatest when the drag is strongest. In this diagram, the bait is being fished off bottom, the usual opening gambit on still waters. The float does, however, permit the presentation of a laid-on bait. To produce the greatest sensitivy in this situation, the shots should be moved as follows. Shot B should be moved down to join shot A, the pair being some 20 inches from the hook. The float should be moved up the line to take account of the increased depth needed to permit A and B to rest on the bottom. At the same time, the bulk shot (C) may also need moving down the line to, at most, a distance of 18 inches below the float. The factors which decide this are depth and drag. The greater either or both of these are the nearer to 18 inches below the float these shot should be set. The back shot (D) is still necessary but you will probably find you can make it smaller, even as small as a dust, for it to still function correctly. One other thing will have happened as a result of these changes: because two of the shots shown in Fig. 10, A and B, are now resting on the bottom instead of being suspended, the reduced pull of weight on the float will mean that more of the tip will show at the surface. Now there'll be ¾ inch instead of the ½ inch indicated in the diagram. Despite this extra show, you may find when the drag is extreme that the float will tend to pull under. The cure for this annoying development is simply to remove some of the bulk shot (C). Also important in this setting is the different behaviour of the float. As set in Fig. 10, most bites are simple submersions. In the laid-on position, the float lifts first before finally submerging. The important thing is to resist the very real temptation to strike at that first lift. Instead, accept it as a warning before the submersion which is the real signal for the strike.

Pause now and think about some of the things I have just been discussing and, once again, you will see you have evidence of different progressions and variation in the indication of bites. Learning these and, more important still, getting used to them is vital for only in this way will you eventually arrive at the situation where you react to such indications instinctively. When you are reading bites instinctively in this way, you will know you have really arrived as a float angler!

4 The Sliding Peacock Antenna and the Missile

In this chapter, I want to consider the still and sluggish water eventualities which we have not covered so far: the need to fish at depths greater than the length of the rod (let's say 10 feet and beyond), the need to fish at extreme range (45 yards and beyond) and, finally, the need to do both these things at once. Without in any way wishing to seem boastful, I think it would be fair to say that this is one field in which I may consider myself a pioneer. Certainly, I'm proudest of the developments I brought about which led to sliding floats and the ability they give us to float fish at extreme depth.

In an effort to tell the story as logically as possible (for that's the way it will be understood most easily), let's begin with the first of the eventualities mentioned above, the need to fish at depths greater than the length of the rod.

To explain this best, I don't think I could do better than ask you to think back over all the floats mentioned so far and pose the question: what, if anything, was the limiting factor about all of them? The answer, and I hope you got it without me telling you, was the depth of the water. All the floats discussed so far were fixed floats. At 10 feet and beyond, they'd be difficult to cast and at 12 feet and beyond, next to impossible.

In the past, the answer for many in this situation was to switch to the leger. On certain occasions, this could be the correct thing to do. On many others, I maintain, it wouldn't and this is where a sliding float is your deep water answer.

What is a sliding float? It is a float which can slide freely up and down the line but which is finally held in the desired position by the ring homing on a stop knot fixed at the desired depth and capable of passing through the rod rings on the cast in a way which will not impede the flow of the tackle to its desired destination—a simple enough statement but one which, in terms of producing the right float for the job, was some years in the achieving.

But as I quickly discovered when I first began detailed experiments with sliders, there are other advantages almost as great. Because of the size of the float and the shot they can carry, they enable a bait to be fished deep, at long distances, both on and off the bottom.

With the sliding antennas, which are fixed at the bottom only, they enable the line to be buried completely in a way which beats the wind and the surface drag.

Compared to legering, casting is much less effort and—a point which should appeal to matchmen—much less time is taken in getting the tackle set in the water ready to signal bites—which, incidentally, present no more resistance to a taking fish than would a simple Crowquill.

The water *needn't* be deeper than your rod before you resort to slider fishing. With a fixed float, there always comes a time when the depth gets critical in terms of the length of your rod. Not only is casting difficult when you reach this stretch point but you commonly find the float being tangled up with the top ring on the retrieve.

The slider can come to your rescue here for more comfortable and efficient fishing. For instance if I was using a 12 foot rod and the water was 10 feet, I'd consider a slider rather than struggle on with a fixed float. Nevertheless, there are limits and in my experience I would say don't use a slider at depths of *less* than 8 feet.

Though it's more than twenty years since I finalised my experiments with sliding floats, today I am more than ever convinced that this principle, once established, was one of the greatest single breakthroughs in the history of float fishing.

It opened up whole new horizons for all anglers. In all honesty I find myself incapable of imagining any new development in float fishing which will achieve as much in one fell blow as the slider did.

It certainly revolutionised my fishing and what's more put me in the match prize money many more times than I might have been.

And now for the sliders themselves, floats which many anglers still seem to have difficulty in understanding. And yet the technique is not only useful but extremely simple—given a little thought and practice.

Perhaps the best way of putting the message across to you is to tell you something of the early days of the sliders and how they came to be perfected.

Almost inevitably it was the drive of matchmen wanting to extend their techniques that led to it all, Coventry matchmen in particular.

Their first research, as I recall it, came in the months which led up to the 1955 National Championship, due to be fished that year in Somerset on the Huntspill River and the King's Sedgemoor Drain.

None of us were keen on legering for the bream there so you can imagine how excited we were when one of our 'spies' returned from Somerset with the news that the locals were getting results with the bream with a form of sliding float.

Within days we'd obtained some of these floats. They were fixed to the line top and bottom by two rings only slightly smaller than the normal pattern with two valve rubbers threaded on between the rings to act as a kind of brake.

To me, the float was crude but it worked—though not very efficiently. When I say this I don't mean to knock my still unknown Somerset friends for they were at least having a go at a difficult problem. Their efforts were certainly the spur which drove me on to experiment.

There were two big troubles with this early slider—it didn't always slide into position properly and it offered enormous resistance on the strike. The Coventry team, including yours truly, liked the idea but not the way it was done. Furious experiments began to try and improve on the float with the idea of beating the Somerset locals at their own game.

After several weeks the best we'd come up with was a porcupine quill with two rings at top and bottom, offset on opposite sides of the float. This, too, worked after a fashion but, like the original from Somerset, it was like hitting a brick on the strike.

Time slipped by quickly and, reluctantly, we decided the idea wasn't good enough yet to justify pinning our faith on it in the National. Instead we used duckers to come second in the match, Coventry's best-ever result up to that time and one we were far from ashamed of for the winners, Sheffield Amalgamated, set up a team weight record for the event that stands to this day.

The sliding float idea was temporarily forgotten—but not by me. I was convinced there were great possibilities so I continued to experiment. And the first thing I did was to forget about porcupine quills. I had already developed the resistance I mentioned earlier to porcupine quills for float making but as you'll discover, while I found my first answer to slider problem elsewhere, I later returned to the 'porcy' for a different but equally useful reason.

Having done so well with Duckers at the National I decided that this shape might be the answer. After many experiments I finally perfected the sliding antenna.

The big problem was always the accurate stopping of the float at the required depth. I had heard of valve rubbers and even matchsticks being used but I wasn't keen. I felt a knot of some kind was the best answer.

It wasn't the biggest breakthrough—that was reserved for a decision to fix the float at the bottom end only and with a tiny ring. I can't remember exactly how it dawned on me but I do recall that the moment I thought of it I felt like saying 'Hey presto!'

Making those first rings—they had and still have a diameter of 0.015 inch (i.e. 15/1000ths of an inch)—had my family in stitches. First I borrowed a needle from the wife's sewing box and fixed it in a vice. Then I made the ring by winding 20 pound alastacum wire tightly around the needle.

It seemed a crazy, footling thing to do but it worked. Incidentally, I tried smaller gauge wire but it was no good. It wouldn't stay in place.

While all this was going on I was also experimenting with materials. I finally chose cane for the stem and balsa for the body. Correctly shotted the float gave three different positive settings, all of which told me that the sequence of events was going the way I wanted it.

Considerably elated, I was still uncertain. As a match angler I needed to succeed with the new idea in the testing conditions of a contest before I could really convince myself that all had gone as well as I had thought.

The first match in which I tried the newborn slider was a Coventry A.A. contest fished by more than 400 on the North Bank of the River Nene. I didn't win—but I was still over the moon for I came second with more than 22 pounds of bream and the winner had only just pipped me by 5 drams!

That was all I needed. I not only knew the float would work but that it was also capable of winning matches. From then on I fished it with all the confidence in the world, winning many matches and being highly placed in many more.

That float was like a live thing to me in that Nene match. I can remember its every movement as if it was some kind of long distance puppet doing just what I wanted it to. First it would lay flat on hitting the water. Next it would spring up and settle to its first setting. The bulk shot had drawn the stop knot to the float rings. Then finally, as the bottom tell-tale went down, the float settled just a little bit farther into the water.

Seconds later it vanished as the first bream took hold. Nothing like a good fish with the first cast of a match!

Even then I remember thinking that this first fish might have been a fluke. I was still on edge when I re-cast. But not after I had netted six of 'em. I was on top of the world and on this particular occasion didn't care a damn whether

I won the match or not. The confidence I got from the slider that day has never left me.

Having, I hope, persuaded any doubters about the true merits of the slider, let's take a more detailed look at the float itself. In its first form (that described in earlier editions of this book), it had a cane stem and a long, slender balsa body. Today, I use a different material—peacock quill—for the stem. Machined to form a really slim tapered antenna, I find this has increased the sensitivity of an already sensitive float. It is also why I now refer to this particular slider as the Sliding Peacock Antenna. As was the case with the original cane and balsa float, it is equipped with that vital 0.015 inch ring at its base.

These days, I find four sizes of this float adequate for all eventualities. The first is 9 inches from tip to base and will carry the equivalent in weight of one swan shot-plus. The others: 10 inches (two swan shot-plus); 11 inches (three swan shot-plus) and 12 inches (four swan shot-plus). Whenever possible, use the smallest float bearing in mind that two factors call for an increase in size, the need to beat a stronger wind when casting and the need to speed the descent of the bait in particularly deep water. The latter point leads me to another truism about sliders: always use enough shot to ensure that the line is drawn *positively* through the smaller float ring now being used.

The next thing you must learn if you are to fish any sliding float correctly is how to tie the stop knot. For reasons which escape me, this knot seems to have puzzled more anglers than any other when, in fact, it is extremely simple. And if you find this hard to believe let me tell you here and now that I couldn't possibly count the thousands of times I've had to demonstrate this knot in recent years— sure proof, I think you'll agree, that this small but vital subject has been fogbound for far too long.

Thanks to our diagrams, I hope you'll find the final end to this knotty problem. They are the finest I have seen— they really explain the knot in the simplest possible way.

It may sound as though I am taking this all a bit too

seriously but if the diagrams and instructions are understood as easily as I think they will be, then I shall literally be relieved of thousands more demonstrations of this knot. And frankly, I can do with the time that would be saved.

So, first look at the diagrams (Figs 11, 12 and 13) carefully and then have a bash yourself. Take a piece of nylon line—about 6 inches is just right—and form it into a U-loop. Lay this alongside the reel line and then pull one end over to form a loop, the position in the first of the three diagrams.

The next step is simply to wind this end over the reel line four or five times and then thread it through the loop that is left (second diagram). By pulling the two ends of the piece of nylon tight you should end up with the knot in diagram 3. Simple, isn't it?

Now I suggested you use a piece of nylon 6 inches long for this job--and for an extremely important reason. A knot with short ends would stop a sliding float moving from its required position on the line. But what a snag you'd find it on the cast as, one after the other, it caught like a brake on every ring on your rod.

By having longer ends this difficulty is completely eliminated. For the smallest sliding float I'd trim the ends to not less than 1 inch; for the bigger ones, 2 inches.

Now to correct another misapprehension about this knot which I've read several times in the past, namely that the knot shouldn't be pulled too tight or it will kink the line. If you've tied it right, this is nonsense!

Believe me, that knot wants to be as tight on the reel line as you can get it, especially with the bigger floats. When the reel line is slack, it should be virtually impossible to move the knot.

Hold the reel line tight and the knot will move easily up and down it. So don't be scared. Pull that knot tight and then carry out this test as a double check. After a few times you'll do all this automatically.

Next another small but important topic which I haven't referred to so far, plumbing the depth. I have left it until

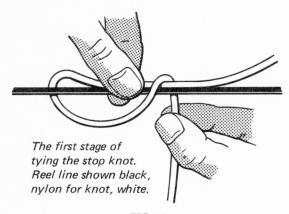

The first stage of
tying the stop knot.
Reel line shown black,
nylon for knot, white.

FIG. 11

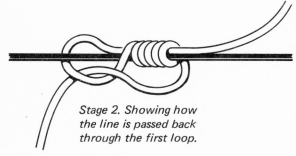

Stage 2. Showing how
the line is passed back
through the first loop.

FIG. 12

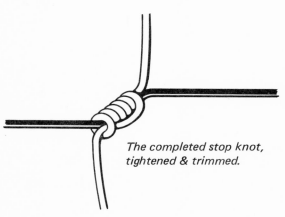

The completed stop knot,
tightened & trimmed.

FIG. 13

now because there is no float where there is greater need for accuracy in plumbing than with the Sliding Peacock Antenna.

Consider first the way you should do this job when fishing with a fixed float.

After fitting the float to the line by looping the line through the ring as described earlier, fix a plummet to the hook. Set the float at what you estimate the depth of the water to be and cast in. Hold your rod up and watch what happens. If the float fails to appear on the surface, this means that you have underestimated the depth and that the water is deeper than you thought. Retrieve the tackle and move the float further up the line. Re-cast and if, this time, the float does show only to lie flat on the surface, this means that the tackle is set to fish too deep. You now know, however, that to get the right setting the float must be moved back down the line but not as far as it was when you made your first cast. By trial and error, you will soon arrive at the correct depth.

The difference with the slider is that as the float is no longer fixed but capable of sliding up and down the line, it is the stop knot which you set at the point you consider equivalent to the depth of the water. With the stop knot set and the plummet in position, cast in and wait to see if the slider shows. If it doesn't, this again means you have underestimated the depth. Furthermore, I always plumb the depth with a slider with the necessary shots in position. So, with the stop knot set, the shots in their place (I'll tell you exactly where in a moment) and the plummet in position, cast in and wait to see if the slider shows. If it doesn't, this again means you have underestimated the depth. The answer now is to move the stop knot further up the line. When you find the true depth, fix the float accurately. It's to achieve this that I do my plumbing with this float with the shots in position. The aim is to set the depth with just an inch of the float tip showing, a reading which tells you all the shot are where they should be, off the bottom.

But do remember to take account of the fact that you

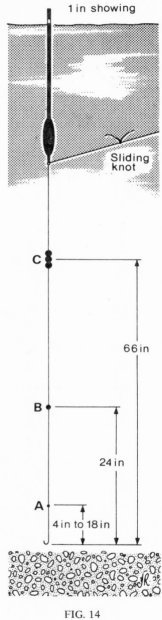

FIG. 14

obtained this reading with the plummet in position. When you remove the plummet, you'll find it necessary to move the stop knot an inch or two nearer the hook to compensate for the previous pull of the plummet to ensure that all the shots are still off bottom.

Let's now consider the shotting pattern itself (Fig. 14). In earlier editions of this book, readers wrote to tell me they found the shotting pattern for the cane and balsa version of this float complicated though, happily, they seemed to get it right in the end. The good news this time is that, thanks to the improved design which is the Sliding Peacock Antenna, I have found it possible to simplify the shotting pattern without in any way reducing the efficiency of the float. In Fig. 14, the float is set to fish just off bottom, the usual starting position with this tackle. Now before I take you on a detailed look at the pattern, let me refer again to the description of the weightings I gave for the various sizes of these floats earlier in this chapter, i.e. one swan shot-plus, two swan shot-plus etc. What I meant, and it's important and best to define it here, is that with the one swan float, that's the weight needed to pull the line positively through the eyelet ring. The plus are the other shots over and above a swan needed to make the tackle fish. The same, of course, goes for the two, three and four swan shot patterns. The first shot on our diagram (A) is the bite tell-tale. This can be as small as a dust shot if you wish though I would suggest you go heavier if there's any wind about to guard against back tangles. B is the stabiliser which finally settles the tackle and C are the bulk which speed the bait down through the water.

A little tip about bulk shot here (and this applies to all floats which call for shots pinched on touching each other in this way) is to pinch them on so that all the slits in the shots are in line with each other. Failure to do this can result in these shots tangling round each other and tying themselves in nasty little knots.

And just to remind you where to put it, the stop knot is shown a little distance up the line from the float. When the tackle is being fished, however, this knot is tight to the float ring.

Now another change from previous editions of this book which, I'm sure, will be a welcome one. In earlier editions, I insisted that cast with this rig should be smooth and underhand, the latter being necessary, I said, so that each part of the tackle would enter the water in its appointed order. This is no longer necessary. Thanks to the new design and the simplified shotting pattern, you can cast this float underhand, overhand or from the side. The only thing you *must* do if there is a wind is to work to the guidelines given in Fig. 8 during our discussion of the Onion float.

What happens *after* the tackle has reached the baited area is just as important. With the shots placed as shown in Fig. 14, the float behaves in ways which, if you watch them carefully, tell you everything is going to plan downstairs. It works like this.

When the float hits the water, it should lie flat. That's because the shots are still pulling line through the small eyelet ring which has not yet engaged with the stop knot. While this is happening, leave the bale arm on your reel open for this will make the line's passage through the ring easier.

The moment the knot reaches the ring, the float will rear up and settle in the water. This is the signal to re-engage the bale arm and it also tells you that the bulk shot (C) are in their required position. When shot B reaches its position, the float will sink a little further finally settling with the weight of shot A so that just an inch of the antenna is showing. Learn to watch carefully for all these movements and get used to the interval between them. If you think any one of the three settings has taken longer than it should, strike, for that means a fish may have taken the bait as it was still falling after the first registration, that is of the bulk shot (C).

If all three settings pass without incident, dip your rod tip under the surface and give a few turns on the reel to make sure the line is buried under the water and out of the way of wind and surface drag, this being a necessity whenever you are fishing any float fixed loose.

Mostly, you will find that fishing the bait just off bottom as shown in the diagram produces most results but there are times when the bait is more likely to be taken when it is laid on. To achieve this setting, move the stop knot up the line so that the bait but *not* shot A is on the bottom. You can tell if you have got it right by watching the float tip. If more is showing than the inch you had before, this means that shot A is, in fact, on the bottom, the loss of its resistance being the reason why more of the float is peeping out of the water.

In the laid-on position, the bite is once again more likely to be of the lift variety. In this same position, you may also find that the drag becomes so extreme the float tip will not hold up out of the water which is where it must be if you are to see bites. The answer is to go in for a light form of float legering.

Fit a Hillman lead—never more than a ¼ ounce and preferably less—on the line above shot A. At the same time move the shots at B and C a couple of feet *up* the line. The presence of the Hillman will compensate for any casting difficulties.

This variation of the rig does have disadvantages and you may find that even with the Hillman on, the float will still drag under. The answer to this is to take some of the bulk shot at C off the line altogether—the amount being that needed to make sure the float still gives its normal 'show'.

The Sliding Antenna, then, is a versatile piece of equipment but it does have its limitations. It should never be used in water with even the suggestion of a stream. Still or extremely sluggish waters are the *only* kinds in which it will work properly.

It has the advantage that a bait can be fished just off the bottom at considerable distances in water which is well over the length of the rod. This advantage, to my mind, is at its best in bream waters whereby fishing off bottom you will still interest the bream but dissuade the eels which can be such a nuisance in this setting.

Furthermore it is the perfect wind and drag cheater.

One last point that bears repeating—despite the fact that you are often using a fair amount of shot and a largish float, the fish will still only feel shot A. Any species can be caught on this tackle from the smallest of roach to the biggest of bream.

Understand the tackle and what it is trying to do before you use it and you are half way there. The most important things about learning to use it correctly are mastering the tying of the stop-knot and getting accustomed by instinct to the behaviour of the float as it goes through its different settings. Both rely completely on accurate plumbing at the outset.

A little practice after that and the Sliding Antenna becomes a new weapon which will bring you more and more fish.

For those who want it to be, the Sliding Peacock Antenna can be more than just a float for tackling extreme depths of water. It can be used to fish any water which is more than 6 feet deep when distance casting is involved. Think about it. You are on a strange still water. You don't know its depth but you are reasonably certain it's not less than 6 feet. If you put this float on from the start, you are set for any depth from 6 feet onwards, a factor which means that, if you are prepared to master it, this one float could do the job of several others we have already discussed (i.e. the Onion or the Mini-Missile) as well as the deep water task for which it was originally designed. It's in its general setting that this float is also far superior to the Zoomer because it's more stable and therefore not prone to the random submersions I mentioned in discussing the latter.

Let's consider the next eventuality mentioned at the beginning of this chapter, the need to fish at extreme ranges of 45 yards and beyond, and the float one must use to cope with this eventuality, in still or sluggish water. Such a float is the Missile. Not only will it fish at the kind of range I have mentioned but, as you will discover, it will also take care of the third and last eventuality I mentioned, the need

Which is the right float for the job? Billy ponders the question
before fishing Dam Flask Reservoir near Sheffield.

Once upon a time all floats were made by hand. Today modern
machines have been adapted to speed the process because of the ever
increasing demand — especially for the patterns recommended by
Bill. This machine produces balsa bodies for floats almost as fast
as you can blink.

Billy plays a lively chub on the Thames near Tadpole. With the wind downstream he used a bodied waggler float fixed bottom only.

A bumper bag of Shannon bream taken by Bill at Lanesborough with an Avon float.

Billy fishes for carp on the delta of the River Ebro in Spain. The float was a Mini-Missile.

Smiles from Billy (left) and Robert Tesse, the Frenchman who is the only man to win the World Championship three times. Billy had just completed a demonstration for Robert of his sliding float technique when this picture was taken and Robert was suitably impressed because the tackle proved sensitive enough to catch the kind of tiddler seen in the picture.

During his career, Bill probably won more 'pots' than any other angler. He's on his way here to set up a special display of them.

Bill swings in a small perch taken at close range from an inviting swim which he fished with a small Avon float.

Always the centre of any angling occasion, this is Bill being interviewed for the telly by angling commentator Alan Wrangles (left).

Bill in action in the 1967 National Championships on the Relief Channel. Clearly visible is the huge Missile float he designed especially for this match and which has become the basis for much development since.

Billy gets a lesson in bristle float fishing with a pole from his friend Robert Tesse.

This very rare picture is
the only one known of Bill
in action in Luxembourg
when he became the first
Englishman ever to win
the World Championships
in 1963.

Bill trotting for roach
from a weir on
Northumberland's River
Till — the swim being
perfect for the Avon float
he used.

Bill unhooks a stillwater bream taken with Mini-Missile tackle.

Match action for Bill on the lower Welland where he's playing a bream hooked on long range waggler tackle.

to fish extreme depths at range. Again, I think you'll understand the advantages of the float better if I tell you how it came to exist. It resulted during practices staged by the Coventry National team in preparation for the 1967 Championships on the Relief Channel, a deep, wide water in West Norfolk.

We soon found that the new float not only flew through the air with the greatest of ease. It did it mighty accurately, too. During tests, there was naturally a lot of talk about it and one of the chance remarks made at this time led to the float finally being christened.

The remark? 'It goes through the air just like a guided missile!' The general feeling was that to refer to it constantly as the 'guided missile' was a bit too clumsy so we ended up calling it simply . . . the Missile.

At least, it's got a nice 20th century sound to it!

Now as many of you will know, the Missile brought me no luck at all in that ill-fated Championship match. I was one of the hundreds waterlicked on a day which produced the worst ever return for our highly rated Coventry team. But at least I can say now that I came out of that match with a new float which has since proved to be one of the most useful I've ever invented in terms of the specific job it was expected to do.

To help you get the picture more, let's refer back to the Relief Channel. Faced with such a water, most anglers, I suppose, would resort to the leger with a swing tip or bite indicator especially as even the biggest existing floats of the sliding variety just didn't have the flying power to take the tackle the extreme distances required.

But we felt a float was still the answer—if one could be found. This was the general opinion of our team after it became obvious during discussions that several members of the side had been extremely successful on this water with a float with the bait fished on a long, slow drop with light terminal tackle because fish were often located well off the bottom.

Alternatively, by nailing the bait to the bottom with a

leger lead we were running the serious risk of putting the bait *below* the fish and giving ourselves time wasting trouble changing tackle if you wanted to look higher in the water.

The answer then was a float which would carry light terminal tackle as far as we wanted and which could be easily adjusted to fish at various depths. This, we reasoned, would give us the same advantage as the leger men with the added facility of being able to move about the various levels in the water much more easily.

Dare I add, too, that such a float would also bring the indication of the bite much nearer the fish than it would with a tip—a point my opponents of the leger know I feel pretty strongly about and one I have yet to feel calls for any change on my part.

No one is going to tell me that a swing tip angler in a water like the Channel is going to get earlier notice of a bite than an angler fishing with a float directly over the bait—especially at the kind of distances I'm going to be talking about now.

I have also heard it said — and recently, too — that the man who uses a swing tip gets half an hour more fishing time in a five hour match because of the speed with which he can put his bait where he wants it in the water. To me, this is just another red herring and a suggestion I reject completely. For it's my opinion that a good float angler can not only match the 'tipper' for speed, he can beat him! Let's face it, you have only to watch some leger anglers after they have cast and they are taking painstaking seconds—sometimes even minutes—to make sure everything is tight to that lead. The float angler does not have this problem—especially with a weapon like the Missile. He merely casts it out to where he wants it and all the time that bait is falling he is in line for a bite.

The Missile, in fact, solves all the problems I've just mentioned. Its great and most obvious advantage is the ease with which it permits you to cast long distances with little effort — and by long distances I am talking of *at least 50 yards*!

It follows that the Missile can be fished literally as far as you are capable of throwing your groundbait because, believe me, the float will always go further if you want it to.

The dodge is to cast the float *beyond* the baited area winding it back quickly to the bait and thus burying the line *deeply* under the surface to prevent wind and surface drag on the line. When you understand this message, you will realise immediately why the original Missile was 16 inches long.

In other words, it's got all the advantages of the biggest Sliding Antenna multiplied twice over.

At the time the Missile gave us the great casting advantage it did, none of us could throw groundbait 50 yards or more and nor could most leger anglers. But until the Missile came along the leger angler did have a casting advantage. These days, following the introduction of more and more sophisticated catapults, the placing of bait in relation to the position of the hookbait is no longer a problem.

This has also meant a further plus for the Missile user. Once the leger angler's bomb has gone under the surface, he's got a heck of a job placing his bait accurately in the chosen area. The Missile, however, gives you a long range marker buoy for this purpose which is mighty useful on waters like the Relief Channel.

But the Channel is not the only water where the missile can be useful. The lower Great Ouse and the Nene are two more. It would also be fine for distance fishing in lakes and reservoirs where the water was deep. It will fish still or sluggish water but is *useless* in flowing water with any strength to speak of to the current.

In match terms, it's been used with most success so far on the North Bank of the Nene. Two Coventry anglers won matches with the missile *before* the Relief Channel National and I was second in another event also using the float. With these results to go on, I'm sure you'll all see why we had so much faith in it for the Channel.

Once I knew the problems that had to be solved with

the missile float, the shape of the thing became immediately obvious.

Now that first Missile was a monster of a float. The stem was 16 inches long, so long the float had to be carried in two parts, the stem being slotted into the body at the waterside. Since that time, I have re-designed the float and while some examples are still big, all are now one-piece jobs.

I achieved the reduction in size simply by increasing the amount of loading in the body. I find five sizes cope with all the eventualities I am likely to encounter. These are: 10 inch (carrying three AAA shot and capable of being cast 45 yards); 12 inch (three swan, 50 yards); and three at 14 inch. These have different body loadings. The three swan float will throw 50 yards, the two swan, 65 yards, and the one swan, 75 yards. Why, you will ask, do floats carrying less shot cast further? That, as I have said, is because they have heavier loads in the bodies. The latter are made of balsa and the stems, as before, of peacock quill.

The shotting pattern for the Missile (Fig. 15) is the same whether you are fishing it on the slide or not, the float at all times being held in position by the stop knot, again shown here above the float on the line though, in fact, it's tight to the float ring when being fished. The pattern, as you can see, is crude but that doesn't seem to matter at these kind of ranges where the fish seem more confident. A is the usual tell-tale and B are the bulk.

By using the knot all the time, you can fish this float shallow or deep but when you are fishing it deep as a slider, it is essential to use the float which carries the most shot for this means the line is drawn through the float ring more easily and quickly.

The remarks I made about versatility in connection with the Sliding Peacock Antenna also apply here for, when all is said and done, the Missile is simply a giant version of this float allowing you to command an enormous field of water whatever the depth.

Other points of similarity between these two floats which are worth noting are these. The Missile, too, can be used in

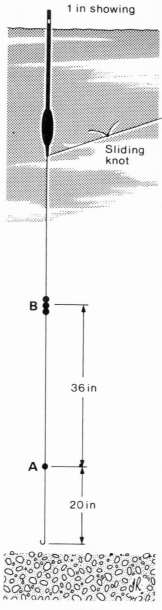

FIG. 15

the laid-on position with, if necessary, shot A actually on the bottom. Like the Sliding Peacock Antenna, it no longer needs to be cast underhand if this doesn't suit you though, again, you must bear in mind the remarks about wind which were coupled with Fig. 8. While the antenna went through three settings in settling in the water, the Missile has two. Lift bites and delayed settings again need watching.

It would be wrong if I was not to add that the need to fish at the extreme ranges with which the Missile will cope is comparatively rare. Nevertheless, no other float will do this job if it *is* required.

Finally, a note of warning. Never attempt to fish a Missile when you are not fishing with it on the slide by fixing loops of line through the ring or by the method favoured by so many when fishing the Waggler, locked shot (see Fig. 16). By doing this, you are putting all the strain of an extremely heavy float on the same part of the line all the time. With the knot, the float rests on the bulk shot at the start of the cast and moves up the line with cast. I have always been opposed to the locked shot system anyway though I prefer to give my reasons for this when we come to discuss the float with which this method has been most associated, the Waggler.

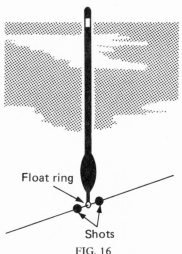

Float ring

Shots

FIG. 16

5 The Avon, the Chubber and the Sliding Chubber

So far in this book, we have considered floats which solve the problems which can face anglers on still and sluggish waters. You will almost certainly have been wondering about fishing rivers and streams: water with some flow to them. In no department of float fishing does one factor, the wind, have a more decisive effect for it's the wind which, from the outset, decides the type of float which can be used.

The most favourable condition for the angler on such waters is when the wind is upstream. This is because the wind acts as a sort of brake on the float, a situation which also enables the angler to ensure that the bait *precedes* the float on its journey downstream. All the floats used in this happy situation are fixed to the line at the top and the bottom, often called double rubber because of the way in which pieces of valve or silicone rubber are used not only to hold the float in place but to permit quick changes to be made.

The most unfavourable condition on these waters is when the wind is downstream. In this circumstance, the wind tends to speed the float on ahead of the bait which, almost invariably, is now *behind* the float in its passage down the river. In an effort to minimise the effect of such winds, all these floats are fixed to the line bottom only so that the angler can bury the line to a large extent below the surface. If a top and bottom float was fished in such a wind, the latter coupled with the surface drag caused by the current will create a huge and largely uncontrollable bow in the line between the rod tip and the float. Taking such a bow out of the line on the strike all too often causes so much delay that the fish is missed. This, then, is one of the main reasons why bottom only floats are used in downstream winds.

Though, as you will discover, anglers do fish stationary baits in the laid-on position in flowing water, the main approach is long trotting, angling parlance for letting the bait run through underneath the float with the speed of the water.

To help you understand why you should use a certain float in certain conditions in a river setting, I think it best to begin by considering first the floats which apply in the most favourable circumstance, when the wind is upstream.

One of the floats we have already discussed can be used in this situation, the Crowquill, but, as I said earlier, conditions have to be absolutely perfect to enable one to fish this float, a statement which means that this is rarely possible.

Think, therefore, of the Crowquill as a limited float in this setting, being careful to restrict its use strictly to the limits I gave earlier. This restriction means, of course, that we must look for something sturdier then the Crowquill, something which could be described as a general purpose float for the conditions we seek to beat. My own personal preference, and certainly the float I would recommend to any beginner, is theAvon. They are not new. In fact, they've been with us so long they can be considered one of the classic patterns but that in no way means that they are 'old hat'. In my view, they are as good today as ever they were which is why I stay faithful to them. I've lost count of the number of match awards these floats have won for me or, for that matter, the number of pleasure outings when they have proved the perfect trotting float. Let me tell you now what they are and more precisely why I like them so much.

They are, so far as I can discover, named after the Warwickshire Avon, which I imagine is the water where they were first found to be so effective. Certainly, it happened before my time!

Since those early days, the Avons have gone on to prove their usefulness in streamy waters, big and small, all over the country: the Severn, Trent, Thames, Tweed, to name just four fairly widespread waters at random.

When I first wrote about these floats in *Angler's Mail* I said they were best made with a crowquill stem which carried a cork body near the thick tip of the float. At the time it was a good combination for in using these materials like this we found that to the general sensitivity of the crowquill cork was adding greater buoyancy at the top—a vital need as I see it for long-trotting, especially in rougher conditions.

The cork, of course, also meant something else when the float was compared with a simple quill. It would carry more lead. These two factors made this the perfect float for the job giving complete control over tackle and bait at all times.

The cork was fighting to keep the tip at the surface while the shot used to give you control over your terminal tackle was trying to pull it down. And while these principles are still most important the Avons—and the Duckers which we are to consider later—have changed for we have been forced to find new materials for making them and, in doing so, have discovered ways of making them fish more efficiently than before.

Like so many of the important developments in fishing it was something of an accident. None of us had any thoughts about changing these floats until we had to. And the reason was simple. We suddenly found that there was a nation-wide shortage of crowquills in the medium and large sizes needed for making these floats correctly, a shortage which was particularly acute with the larger quills.

So bad did things become it became obvious we were going to have to find different materials for making these floats if we were going to be able to continue using them.

And this took time. At first we found we could still, if we were extremely lucky, obtain some crowquills but, almost without exception, they turned out to be on the small side when it came to using them for the manufacture of Avons and Duckers and all our attempts to continue making the floats with these quills merely ended up with float stems which tended to break on the strike.

At the same time, there were some larger quills about but these turned out to be from sea birds and, as I am sure you will notice immediately if you examine them yourself, you will see that they do not have the same streamlined shape of the crowquill, a shape which, to me, has always been one of the essential advantages of this material for making floats of the type we are discussing. We also found, incidentally, that it was next to impossible to get the cork body to fit properly on these sea bird quills in a way which would make the float give the correct 'show' in the water.

Next we tried that old favourite for some, porcupine quill, but here again there were problems. Because their diameters varied so much the job of fitting the float body to them became a nightmare or just plain impossible.

In the end, I decided that the best way of solving the problem was to dispense with the use of quills altogether and to begin looking for something else which, one hoped, would serve the same purpose.

And the answer we finally came up with was cane for the stem, and balsa for the body, both materials which gave us the ability to work to exactly the size we wanted with every float.

The float tip above the balsa body is stubbier than it was (a change which now permits checking of the float in a way which wasn't possible before) while the stem below the body remains the same. The body is shaped balsa and after being slid on to the cane is glued, the whole thing being painted and thoroughly varnished to make it watertight.

Now all this meant that, for the first time, we could make Avons and Duckers exactly the same size every time —a thing which was impossible with crowquills for the stem and cork for the body.

With these latter materials there was always a variation

in the floats, a variation which could often mean that the shot carrying capacities of two floats which seemingly looked exactly the same size could often differ with, say, a medium size Avon, by as much as an AAA shot. In other words, every one of these floats had to be individually shotted beforehand if one was to be able to use them speedily and efficiently.

It should follow that because the new Avon and Duckers made with cane and balsa are capable of being made exactly the same size the shotting capacity of every one of them in each particular size is precisely the same and their accuracy can be absolutely relied upon. So, apart from solving a problem caused by the shortage of a once vital material, this is our first bonus—a group of floats which can be accurately shotted as a group for the first time.

But, as we came to use the floats made from these new materials more often, we quickly found that there were further gains in terms of their efficiency.

Most important is that we now have much greater control over the buoyancy of the float. With the old Avons and Duckers the cork body *had* to go where it fitted tightest on the quill stem for the float to be fished satisfactorily. The trouble with this, particularly with the Avons, was that there was all too often a longer antenna or tip above the cork body than there needed to be, a factor which distinctly interfered with the 'show' of the float, the presentation of the bait, and the control of the float.

With the new material—cork and balsa—we can fit the body of the Avon much nearer the tip because we are no longer governed by the diameter of the quills which were used before. And, of course, we can put it in the same place every time and this also means that we can make the tip thicker or thinner at will so that the buoyancy of the float —the relation of tip and stem to body—is perfect.

Another bonus is that the 'show' of the Avons and Duckers now is much prouder in the water than it was before without in any way interfering with the sensitivity of the tackle, an advance of the greatest usefulness.

The fact, too, that we are now able to exactly control the diameter of the float stem also helps give us better control when actually fishing especially in fast water. The old style Avon, however well you fished it, had a nasty habit of tending to rise up in the water on checking, a thing which could, of course, disturb the bait in such a way that it could cost you a bite. The new cane and balsa job doesn't have this habit to the same degree, if at all.

These days, I find five Avons adequate for all my needs. Their length and their shot carrying capacities are: 5½ inches (two BB); 6 inches (three BB); 6½ inches (four BB); 7 inches (five BB); 6½ inches (4AAA, the extra weight for the shorter length with this float being achieved by fitting a bigger body).

In moving on to the how of fishing an Avon float, I find, since the earlier editions of this book, that, thanks to the new design and materials used for these floats, I have been able to considerably simplify the shotting system I use with them, the new pattern being shown in Fig. 17. To me, this gives added versatility to an already versatile float. The placing of the tell-tale (A) and the reasons for it should, by now, be obvious. It's the position of the bulk (B) which is intriguing. As you can see they can be put anywhere from a point 20 inches above the hook on up to just under the float ring itself. Exactly where they go is decided by the bait being fished. With baits like maggot, worm and bread, 20 inches above A should be fine in a normal flow. If, however, there's real strength to the current, these shots should be moved nearer to A, in extreme currents being pinched on side by side with A. It's when the caster is used that the versatility of the pattern is demonstrated. With this bait, fish respond at varying levels and unless the bait is offered to the fish in a positive manner at the taking level you won't catch them. You need to establish that level and this, in turn, will tell you where to set the shots marked B. Sometimes, you will need them right under the float, this to impart a slow fall to the bait. Sometimes, they'll be midway between A and the float. At others, you may find it necessary to split them with just one under the float and

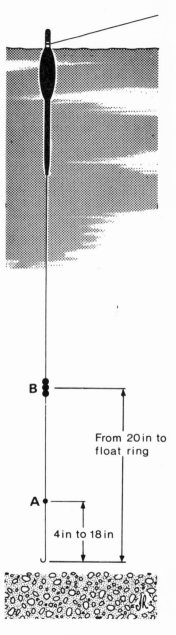

FIG. 17

the other exactly halfway between this upper shot and **A**. Only the behaviour of the fish on the day can finally settle the placement of these shot for you.

Now let me tell you about another facility the Avon offers which was not possible before, the ability (with the shots as in Fig. 17) to check the float. But before describing this process, let me remind you of what I said in earlier editions of this book about ensuring that the bait really does precede the float down the swim. This is what I said. To get the correct flow of the tackle, cast in slightly upstream from the point where your swim begins—and I do mean slightly. Hold your rod high in the air until the float has cocked and begun its journey down the swim. Now bring your rod down, holding it pointing slightly downstream, a position you will retain throughout the float's passage down the swim. By completing these motions—and especially by making sure your line is lying straight to the float when the rod is high—you will ensure that the terminal tackle is travelling correctly. To that, I would only add that it is important to maintain a reasonably tight line between rod tip and float during the trotting process.

I then went on to say the following: it is most important that you don't make any check on the float when it is travelling down the swim for this will jerk the bait and alarm the fish. Thanks to the new shotting pattern and the stubbier, more buoyant tips these floats have, an Avon float can now be checked on its way down the swim. You do this by momentarily halting the flow of line from the reel. This causes the float to pause and, as it does so, the bait lifts and hovers attractively in the water. A bite is often instant at such moments. If, on the other hand, a fish doesn't oblige then simply release the line and allow the float's progress to continue, checking the bait at intervals again as the trot continues. Sometimes, fish will only take a bait on the check. At others, they won't accept it unless it is fished with the speed of the current. Another small tip when you wish to check the float is to move the upper valve rubber down so it is just above the neck of the body.

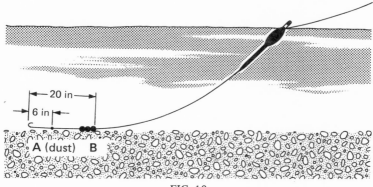

FIG. 18

The next question is: what about laying on or float legering with the Avon? The answer is that the float is excellent for both these methods. In fact, these days I see one of these methods automatically leading to the other. I begin with the tackle set as shown in Fig. 18. The float, as you can see, is set to fish well over the true depth of the water. Just how much over depth you should set it depends on the flow. The greater this is the more float should be moved over depth. Look at the diagram now and you can see that the tell-tale (A) and the bulk (B) are laid on the bottom of the river. With the float shotted in this way, the tackle should be cast out to the baited area. The rod is then placed in a rest pointing at an angle of 45 degrees with the tip to your front and not towards the bait. This helps to keep as much line as possible out of the water, and helps the bait to hold bottom that bit further out from the bank than it might. You could describe what is being done now as a form of stret-pegging, the main difference being that with pegging the bite is shown by a wobbling of the float while with my approach you'll get a clean submersion of the float and that is always more satisfying.

Once I have discovered that the fish in the swim are willing to accept a bait offered in this manner, I change tactics immediately to the simple float leger ring shown in Fig. 19. To set this up, simply tie on a 6 inch length of line to the main reel line 20 inches above the hook. With the float only

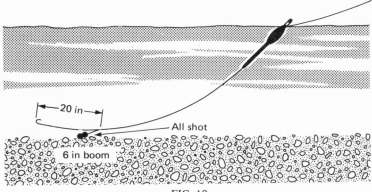

FIG. 19

half as much over depth as you had it for Fig. 18, pinch
onto the extension line (called a boom) exactly the amount
of shot which would normally be needed to cock the float.
Then tie a single knot in the end of the boom to prevent
the shot from slipping off. *At no time* put any shot on the
main line. Cast in and set up the rod as before. You may
find that the float will not hold its position, in which case
simply add more shot, resorting, if necessary, to a leger
weight on the boom instead of shot. The bites are even
more decisive than Fig. 18, a statement which should prompt
you to ask why bother with the tackle in Fig. 18 anyway.
The answer is that if you have been trotting the swim in
the normal way, you can give Fig. 18 a try without changing
the end tackle. If bites don't result, you can go straight back
to trotting. If they do then you know the change is worth-
while. Still another question is why the tackle in Fig. 18
should not produce such positive bites in Fig. 19. The
answer is that, with the second rig, the bite is communicated
more directly to the float, this, of course, being the reason
why I was so insistent that no shot should be put on the
main line.

In extreme conditions of flow, however, Fig. 19 may not
work, in which case it's perfectly all right with the Avon to
use the biggest leger weight you need to hold.

Now a few tips about fishing the heavier Avons with the
speed of the flow as opposed to laying on or float legering.

For starters, you need strong lines. It's no good using 2 pound line with these bigger floats. Line between 3½ and 4½ pounds is best, the latter the heaviest I would go. And now a comment about water where these floats really prove their worth—the famous Hampshire Avon, a river for which some really incredible tackles have been suggested.

I've seen some fabulous monstrosities—none of which could hold a candle to the orthodox version of a big Avon, with the proviso that the chosen swim was free of obstructions on the bottom. Given a clear swim these Avons are *the* tackle boss in the famous Hampshire river.

And even in the weediest water there is, it's still an Avon float you want. I found this out by experience on an entirely different river—the Windrush at Whitney in Oxfordshire. Unknown to me at the time this is rather like a Hampshire Avon in miniature, fast-flowing and with huge clumps of streamer weed.

At first I tried a heavyish Avon float tackle but the leads constantly tangled in the weeds. The answer? I found that by switching to a smaller Avon float—like the one I talked about earlier—it was easily possible to trot the river efficiently without a single tangle, provided that all the weight except the final shot was placed directly under the float.

This piece of information lodged firmly in my mind and when I later went to the Hampshire Avon I found all the same things to be true. The bigger Avon was just fine with a clear bottom. Where there were weeds I simply did a Windrush and switched to a smaller Avon to get complete control of my tackle.

My reservations about the Hampshire Avon, incidentally, offer a good yardstick about when to decide to go heavier with an Avon float. Wherever there is excessive weed growth you want to avoid lead in any quantity on the terminal length.

So the thing to remember when thinking about heavy Avon tackle for heavy water is that you must have a clear run down the swim.

Before moving onto our next float, let me just re-cap on

a few important points of Avon practice. *Never* (and this is the most important consideration of all) use an Avon in a downstream wind. *Never* use them in still water. *Never* at any time when long trotting allow the lower tell-tale shot to touch or drag the bottom. *Never* use the larger sizes with light lines.

Let's go on now to the float I recommend when even the biggest of our Avons won't cope with conditions that, to say the least, will have become distinctly rough—the Chubber. This float replaces the larger Avons which appeared in earlier additions of this book and if you look at its shape in our diagram (Fig. 20), you will see that it is like a truncated Avon, the stem having vanished and the body being increased in diameter.

This float (and it's not the only one of its kind in this book) is designed to carry a lot of weight and, for this reason, I'd like to take it as a cue to digress for a moment and say something about this business of weight when float fishing for it is so important.

So many anglers seem frightened of using weight when float fishing and, over the years, I've often been challenged by such people for the fact that I have no inhibitions in this direction. Indeed, it has been said that I was one of the first to lose my fears under this heading. If that is true I am delighted, for it means I have learned a lesson others seem to be refusing to learn, to their own cost.

What critics of heavy tactics seem incapable of understanding is that it doesn't matter how much weight a float carries provided that weight is balanced in such a way that the fish only feels the resistance of the tell-tale shot. I well remember an occasion in France when I first demonstrated the sliding float principle to my old friend Robert Tesse, the only man, incidentally, ever to become World Champion three times. As you have seen in the last chapter, these floats carry a lot of weight because of the distance they are often required to travel and the need to speed the bait down where it's wanted in deep water. Because that weight has been correctly balanced, however, the fish only ever feel the

A

12 in to 18 in

FIG. 20

bottom shot. Nevertheless, Robert and his friends looked on amazed when I made my first cast away past the range of their longest poles with this rig. The looks on their faces told me that they were convinced this was one demonstration that was not going to have a happy ending. When I started catching small roach and gudgeon every cast at this range, their attitude changed and before that day was out they were still asking questions about the tackle. Wise anglers like these, of course, never neglect the chance to learn something new.

Those who still insist that the tackle must always be light are wrong because they are insisting that the water should accept the tackle they want to inflict on it when the equation should be the other way round. The water and the conditions on the day should dictate the tackle used.

Let me leave this subject with another point. Since that day in 1963 when I won the World Championship only two other English anglers have taken the title, Robin Harris of Peterborough in Germany in 1969 and Ian Heaps of Stockport in Poland in 1975. Both of them are anglers who have never been afraid to fish heavy when conditions demanded it and I'm sure this attitude played a key part in their success.

Back now to the Chubber and if you look at Fig. 20, you will see that, compared with the big Avon rigs I used to use, the tackle, though still heavy to deal with heavy conditions, is much simpler. I use three Chubbers. The first is 3 inches from tip to base and will carry three swan shot. The others are 4 inches (four swan) and 5 inches (five swan). Look now at the shotting pattern and you will see it's simplicity itself with all the floats pinched on at point A like one giant tell-tale. But it's not the strength of bites which decides where they go. That's settled by the bait being used and this float is ideal for offering baits like bread flake, wasp grub, luncheon meat and big bunches of maggots or caster. For bread flake, the shots should be 12 inches from the hook, for all the rest, 18 inches.

Unlike the smaller Avons we have just been discussing,

the Chubber may *not* be checked on its passage through the swim. It *must* be fished with the speed of the water.

Basically, it's all a question of control. Just as with driving a car, you must be in charge. A float tackle which sees you struggling to retain control has got to be wrong. In so many instances, the answer is the extra weight permitted by these bigger floats.

Now some might think a float like the Chubber is a float you'll rarely use. I'll say the reverse, always depending on where you fish. If you're an angler who spends a lot of time on rivers like the Dorset Stour, the Hampshire Avon, the Severn or the Thames, to name but four big streams with strong flows, the Chubber should be on your line regularly.

Now in these rivers, you will find good swims which are very deep, too deep to fish with a fixed float. These will be swims of excessive power with a strong, remorseless undercurrent. Such flows are certainly too strong for the more commonly used sliding float for rivers, the Balsa, which is to be discussed in our next chapter. The answer here is the sliding Chubber. The only difference between this float and the one we have just been discussing is that it has an extra ring on the float tip, this again being only 0.015 inch in diameter so that the float will hold against the stop knot described earlier in Figs 11, 12 and 13. For big baits like bread flake, luncheon meat and wasp grub, the float should be shotted in precisely the same way as that shown for the Chubber (Fig. 20) but when the bait is maggot or caster, I recommend the pattern shown in Fig. 21, the main difference between them being that the bulk shot (A) are placed higher up the line and we have re-introduced a tell-tale shot (B). This gives you a little extra sensitivity coupled with no loss of control for these smaller baits and, as before, the tell-tale goes nearer the hook if bites are hard to hit—something that shouldn't happen in this kind of water where a fish must take positively if it is to take at all.

In the kind of deep water where you would use this float, the lower Severn being most typical, you will find that you get tremendous variations in depth in one swim. It may be

Sliding stop knot

A = Bulk shot
3 AAA +

B = BB

36 in

6 in to 24 in

FIG. 21

18 feet at one point, 16 feet at another and 14 feet at a third. This doesn't matter. With this rig, you will find the bait passes easily over them and in such a way that you do *not* have to constantly mend line causing fish-scaring jerks on the way through the swim.

I should finally warn you that it is not possible to lay on or float leger with this float. When that eventuality seems likely, the only answer in water of this power must be the leger.

Now while I still consider the Avon and its alternative, the Chubber, the best basic floats for tackling running water in an upstream wind, especially for the beginner, there are others which, one must admit, are much more commonly used these days. The Stick is a good example. I have long had doubts about some of them. I still have but, on the other hand, I like to think that I have, at last, got them in their right perspective. Just how is something I'll be dealing with in the next chapter.

6 The Stick, the Wire-Stemmed Stick, the Balsa and the Sliding Balsa

Still in the field of floats for use on streamy water when the wind is upstream, we come first to a float that, for more than a decade now, has been one of the most fashionable of them all, the Stick. As readers of previous editions of this book and my many friends will confirm, I have long had doubts about the claims made for this float and I still have. Yet anglers over the country are still using them, and not a week goes by without one reading of yet another match being won with one. So is it a question of all these anglers being right and pig-headed me wrong? The answer will take some giving but, in the telling, I hope it will give a new and, hopefully, better perspective on this front.

It is in fact, doubtful whether there has ever been a single float which made such a great impact on the angling world as the ubiquitous Stick, a slim float with a cane stem which gets its buoyancy from a carefully built-on balsa tip.

It had its origins in Lancashire and it was here that it first began winning matches. Then the better anglers from Lancashire, men like Benny Ashurst and his son, Kevin, began travelling to rivers like the Trent where they began to win match after match, invariably using the Stick.

Its success was not lost on their competitors who soon began trying the float for themselves and, as the Trent was, and still is, a mecca for anglers from all over the country, news of the Stick travelled fast.

As matches (and more important, money) were involved, everybody started Stick fishing. This is a common thing. As soon as any man starts to do well in matches, others start to copy the things he does in the belief that this will bring them similar success. I know. I have had this happen to me on more occasions than I can remember.

What many of these early Stick copyists overlooked, and it's not surprising because it was a subject on which the North Westerners were not given to being talkative, was that when they were successful with this float, they were also using a particular bait, the then new caster.

The Stick, and the way it was shotted, was totally allied to the caster. Latterly, however, anglers have made it work equally well with maggot and other baits like bread punch though I think it would be true to say it remains very much a float for the match angler, who needs fine presentation on waters where the fish are educated, rather than for the pleasure angler.

Let's consider now the advantages and disadvantages of the Stick.

Its greatest advantage is that it allows very delicate presentation of a bait offered on a small hook (say 18s on down) with fine lines, often as fine as 1 pound for the reel line and 12 ounces for the hook length. These, of course, are great advantages for the match angler who is often seeking small bonus fish though I should add in fairness that today one regularly hears of them subduing bigger things on this kind of tackle.

The main disadvantage with the Stick is that conditions must be absolutely right if it is to succeed. The wind must be a gentle upstream breeze and the swim, usually marginal instead of any distance out from the bank, must have a smooth flowing surface with no boils in it—exactly the kind of benign running water conditions in which earlier I said the Crowquill would work.

So why use a Stick instead of a Crowquill? If the Stick is made with the correct ratio of balsa to cane, the Stick is more buoyant at the tip than the Crowquill and this makes for better control in the long trotting situation between rod and float. Its heavier weight means it will cast further than the Crowquill and, with these advantages, sensitivity is maintained.

In the right conditions on a river, then, the Stick is more efficient than a Crowquill though the latter remains a joy to use and is still *the* float to use in the still water setting described earlier.

For this reason, I have no objection to Sticks provided the conditions are what they demand. Where the reverse is the case they offer nothing like the stability and control you can get from the smaller patterns of Avon.

The fact that so many anglers use Sticks so often suggests to me that many of them are using them when the conditions are not right for them. They have become victims to fashion and are persevering with their Sticks when their interests might best be served by a switch to something more stable.

Let's presume, then, that the conditions are right for the Stick. They can be shotted like an Avon (see Fig. 17) but, without any doubt, the most commonly used system is the now famous string of shot pattern (Fig. 22). This pattern very much grew from the development of the caster as a bait though, as I said earlier, it is now used with other baits like maggot, too. The object of this pattern—and it can be used with other floats—is to make the right things happen downstairs, most especially when you are checking the bait on its way down the swim, this latter, as we have seen, is something which can yield the most decisive bites. Why is this so? Consider now Fig. 23.

The best way of explaining this is for you to imagine first that we have *not* shotted in this manner but have put our bulk shot about 18 inches from the hook. When you hold tackle set like this back in streamy water you get a bow in the line underwater in a downstream direction (see Fig. 23). It follows that if a fish chose to take at this moment it would have to pull the bow out of the line before any indication of its action was shown on the float and this is,

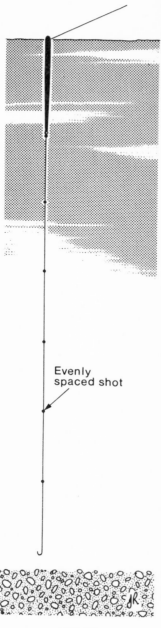

FIG. 22

Evenly
spaced shot

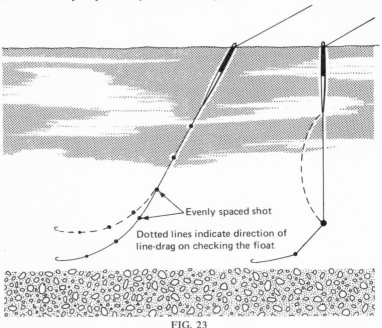

Evenly spaced shot

Dotted lines indicate direction of
line-drag on checking the float

FIG. 23

in fact, the main reason why tackle set like this to interest fish feeding deep should never be held back in this way.

By setting the leads evenly that bow is prevented when the tackle is checked. In this setting the tackle, on checking, merely leads to a natural lifting of the line between float and hook in a downstream direction so that the taking fish still immediately gives a signal on the float.

Now this even method of shotting is, like the float itself, closely tied up with that link between Stick floats and casters. I am, of course, referring to the way in which caster anglers feed their swims. They don't groundbait heavily and on most occasions use none at all.

In waters like the Trent—a typical Stick water—they normally feed 2 pints of casters or more during a match or pleasure stint and they put them in loose so that the fish are taking them at constantly varying depths.

From this it will be clear that the caster angler with his Stick float shotted in the way I have illustrated can attract fish at these varying levels merely by checking the float. In fact, one of the deadliest ways of fishing casters is to use them with the float held back in fits and jerks on its way down through the swim, the system which is now called checking.

The tackle itself is invariably set deeper than the depth which you are fishing to better facilitate this searching action I have mentioned. If, for example, the swim averaged 4 feet in depth, you would set the float 5 feet above the hook.

When you cast you should give the tackle an immediate check which will produce a tight line to your float and make certain that the bait is moving off down the swim ahead of the float and *off* the bottom. When it's released you have a perfect two-way tension between rod and float and shots to float.

Because the Stick is so easy to control this balance created by the line tight to the float gives you a natural hold on the tackle. At the same time it is because this balance is so fine that conditions must be absolutely right for Stick float fishing and therein, of course, lie its limitations. By checking the float at intervals down the swim you can search the water all the time and, I would emphasise, fish will most often take at these moments of checking and you should always be ready at these times.

I cannot advise you to read this last passage too carefully for it gives the key to the relationship between the Stick float and caster fishing. The hovering effect which the checking of the float gives the bait, thanks, as I hope I have demonstrated, to the shotting, is the main reason why this is such a successful rig.

Another reason why evenly spaced shots are such an advantage with casters is that, in my opinion, fish like to take a caster slowly. They like to consider it and, perhaps, mouth it before making the final, fatal chew. This shotting system permits them to do this with no risk of the shots pulling the bait out of the fish's mouth.

Basically, we fish casters with the Stick over-depth to get the best results and, normally, would always begin by fishing in this way. But there is one exception to this and that is where the water is heated by outfalls from such bankside installations as power stations, a thing which occurs often in rivers like the Trent and the Calder.

In this setting fish rarely hang about near the bottom. They are swimming at all depths because of the extreme fermentation and souring which takes place on the bed of rivers in sections like this. And that is why in such places I would think nothing of fishing anything between 1 foot and 3 feet *under* depth. I would still retain that so-important checking ability but would be saving time because I am no longer searching a part of the river which contained nothing.

Some anglers also use Stick floats for still water conditions in which instance they merely fix the float at the lower end instead of top and bottom, a system which is known in some parts of the country as 'pegging'.

I don't like this method myself for I think that the strike is seriously impaired and that, in any case, there are other floats far, far superior for this job, for example the simple Crowquill, the reverse Crowquill, the Onion, the Dart, the Mini-Missiles and the Sliders.

Let me go back now for a moment to our shotting pattern (Fig. 22). Usually, the lowest shot, the tell-tale in this setting, is a dust. The others, evenly spaced as shown, are slightly larger, say No. 6s or No. 4s. Sometimes, however, it's better to have each shot increasing in size on the way from the tell-tale up to the float. Only trial and error on the day will tell you which is best.

The important thing to understand is that the string of shot pattern is not just limited to use with the Stick. It can be used with other upstream wind patterns in running water like the Avon, especially the latter since its design has been improved.

Still with this pattern, however, there has been a recent interesting development which began, I believe, on the Trent. Despite previous reservations (to which I've most definitely been a party), anglers are now using Sticks in a downstream wind, their aim, of course, being to achieve the excellent bait presentation offered by the float with the string of shot pattern in this seemingly adverse condition. The way they are doing it is simplicity itself. They are pinching on a back shot (most often a No. 6) about 8 inches topside of the float. This enables them to achieve a burying of the line between the float and the rod tip. I have not had the opportunity to try this new idea myself but I was greatly intrigued when I heard about it and in view of the reputations of the anglers now using it, it is most definitely something worth trying. Like so many things in angling, it's a simple answer to an obvious question. That it works, I've no doubt, otherwise famous names would not be using it if it didn't. In view of their success, one must now wonder whether the same principle can be applied to other top-and-bottom floats so that they, too, can be efficiently used in downstreamers. It's worth more than a passing thought.

For the sake of progress, let's accept that the swim we are faced with fishing is different. The wind is still pleasantly upstream but there's a certain amount of boil and turbulence in the peg. The answer for the Stick float angler is a change to another form of the same float, the wire-stemmed Stick.

All it is is a slim piece of balsa with a stiff wire stem, piano wire being one of the best materials to use for the latter because it is so rigid. This has, of course, led to a basic change in the nature of the float. In the conventional stick the buoyancy is created by the tug of war between the cane and balsa sections of the float.

With the wire Stick *all* the buoyancy has been centred in the tip which explains why it can cope with rougher waters than the earlier model.

It is also much more stable and because it rides more vertically in the water than the normal Stick it gives a more immediate indication of the bite, a fact which explains why some prefer the wire-stemmed version of this float for all their Stick float fishing.

Shotting with the wire-stemmed Stick is again with the string of shot system (Fig. 22). The Avon system (Fig. 17) can also be used though I prefer the simplified form of this

FIG. 24

shown in Fig. 24 for this float. I regularly use four sizes of wire-stemmed Sticks. The smallest is 6½ inches long, carrying the equivalent of two BB shot. The others: 6¾ inches (three BB); 7 inches (four BB) and 7¼ inches (five BB).

Shotting with Sticks has generally to be extremely exact and most anglers I know have a code of markings for their collection of Stick floats which enables them to shot them up correctly at a glance. This is a system I would urge anyone to copy.

Now one last point before I sum up about these floats. Laying-on, in the true sense of the phrase, is not really possible with the stick. By this I mean that you lay-on—but with a difference. The even spaced shotting pattern remains the same and the float is set to fish 50 per cent over depth but when the tackle is in the water you don't, as you normally would, let it lie still for long periods. You cast, let it pause, and then allow the bait to move downstream; another pause, and then repeat the operation.

To sum up about Sticks, don't use them when the wind is downstream or in your face. Don't use them in still waters. Don't use the conventional cane and balsa stick in turbulent swims. Never be afraid to check the tackle during trotting. Always maintain a tight line between rod tip and float when doing so.

There comes a stage, of course, when even the wire-stemmed Stick will not do the necessary. Usually, this is when the swim has a bit of depth and power to it and, to cope, a float is needed that will carry more weight so as to get the bait down to fish in a way that makes sure it stays there. The Stick float angler's answer these days is the Straight Balsa, called in some parts of the country, a Glider. Your Avon fan in this situation would, of course, simply change to a bigger float. The Stick angler, especially if he is a matchman, maintains that the Balsa is the best alternative and, these days, it's hard to quarrel with that attitude in view of the results being achieved.

As its name suggests, the Balsa is made entirely of round balsa wood. As a float, it was known long before the Stick,

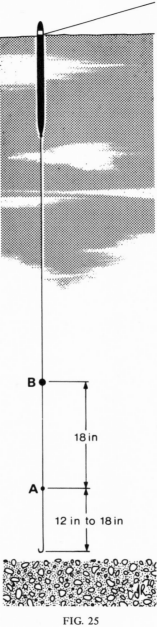

FIG. 25

having been introduced, to the best of my knowledge, as a substitute for the tangle-prone porcupine quill. It was lighter than the porcupine quill with the result that, on the cast, the shots travelled ahead of the float and were, therefore, less likely to tangle. These days, you hardly ever see a porcupine quill, thanks to the Balsa.

The disadvantage of the Balsa is that because it is so buoyant it can offer difficulties in terms of control. To explain this best, I can only suggest you trot a Balsa through a swim and check it and you will find it reacts violently in the way it veers off course. These days, however, the Stick man switching to the Balsa does not fish the float with the speed of flow. He invariably holds it back *all the time* so that it is going down the swim under resistance from the reel. Sometimes, he'll stop it altogether and, often, that turns out to be the moment for the bite. It follows from this that a float fished in such a way must be fished over depth, and that the shots on the end are not so heavy they do not permit the bait to lift off the bottom so as to pass over any obstructions there as it is carried along by the current's force. The simplest shotting pattern for the Balsa is that shown in Fig. 25. With this you would be trying to fish with the speed of flow. You can also use the string of shot system (Fig. 22), the Balsa allowing you to present it in stronger water than the Stick. A third alternative is the system shown in Fig. 26 which, if you look at it carefully, is virtually the string of shot system applied to the lower end of the tackle only except that it is essential in this setting that the shots increase in size as shown. This is the system to use with the Balsa when you are fishing the hold back technique which is now the most commonly used with this float.

Finally in this chapter, I come to another float which has replaced one of the old faithfuls which appeared in previous editions of this book: the sliding Porcupine, the float which coped with water deeper than the rod when the wind was upstream. We have already seen an example of a float that will perform this function in the last chapter, the sliding Chubber, but that, I hope you will recall, was

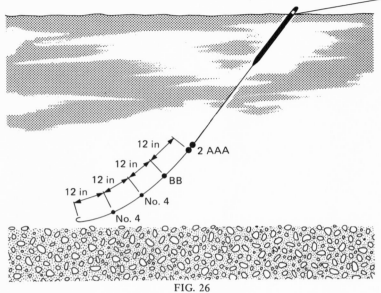

FIG. 26

for really powerful swims. The sliding Porcupine and now its successor, the sliding Balsa, is the float to use in any normal streamy water swim which is deeper than your rod will comfortably handle.

I changed to balsa as the material for this float for the same reason that so many anglers had earlier changed to it from porcupine quill, to guard against tangles round the tip which were always likely with porcupine quills. In addition, I kept finding that unless I used a really huge quill, the float would not carry the weight I needed to get the bait quickly down and fishing in running water. Now balsa, as I said earlier, will take a lot of weight and size-for-size, a float made up of this material will certainly take more weight than one of the same size made of porcupine quill.

And so I arrive at the pattern of float you see in Fig. 27. As you can see the line passes first through a small eyelet ring (0.015 inch diameter again) at the top and down through the ring at the base of the float. As before, it is held in the desired position by a sliding stop knot. With this float, we'll be fishing water 10 feet deep and more. The tell-tale (shot **A**) varies in the size, the message here

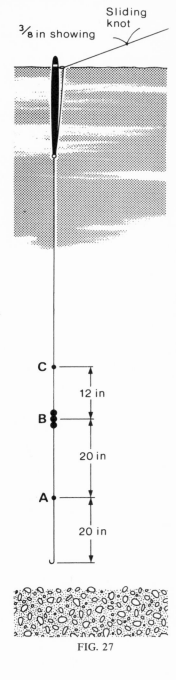

FIG. 27

being that the stronger the flow is, the larger this shot should be, up to a maximum of a BB. The bulk shot (B) are there to speed the bait down and to ensure that the line passes smoothly through the float rings to engage the stop knot as quickly as possible. Shot C is a stop shot used to keep the float clear of the bulk shot on the cast, another precaution designed to reduce the possibility of back tangles. The main tip I would give is to be sure to use enough bulk shot to ensure the line passes quickly through those rings and, to speed this up, you should hold the rod up so as to assist this process. Think about it. If you let the line just dawdle through those rings, the tackle could have passed clean through the taking area before the bait was fishing where it's needed . . . deep down in the water.

Think, too, about the different settings which are always there to tell you a story when slider fishing. The first with this float comes when the bulk shot engage the stop shot, the second being when the weight of the tell-tale is felt.

The big difference between this float and the sliding Peacock Antenna which is fished bottom only is that by watching carefully after the cast, you can see, because the line is on the surface and not buried, a small wake running along the surface. It's worth watching for as it tells you beyond any doubt that the line *is* travelling smoothly between the float rings and that everything, therefore, must be working equally well below. Spot the wake and leave the bale arm of your reel open until the knot engages and you are ready to react to anything that might develop with the first setting of the float.

There is one other very important bonus to the sliding Balsa. I find I can also fish it when the wind is *downstream*, making this the only top and bottom float I would use in this way, though I would add that it is not as efficient in this kind of wind as it is when the wind is coming up river. Nevertheless, it does help and any gain you can make whenever you are float fishing, as I've tried to demonstrate over and over again in this book, is something you cannot afford to overlook.

7 The Ducker and its Alternatives

Now while the floats we have just been discussing, all fixed top and bottom or, as some would say 'double rubber', are extremely useful in running water, all, as I mentioned earlier, had one big disadvantage. They are no good when the river angler's most disliked condition, a downstream wind, prevails.

The answer is to switch to a float which is fixed to the line at the base only, what most call a 'bottom only' fixture. The immediate advantage of this, as we discovered when considering still water floats, is that it allows the line between rod tip and float to be sunk below the surface out of the way of the wind. After the cast with such a float on a river, the angler usually gives a quick flick of the rod to tighten the line, sometimes coupled with a few turns on the reel. This puts the line out of the way of the wind.

The main disadvantage on a river when a bottom only float is fished is that it cannot be checked. If you do attempt to do this, the float submerges, thus indicating a false bite.

So much for basic principles . . . now for the detail.

In earlier editions of this book, the float I recommended most strongly for this condition was the Ducker, a stubby sort of job with a body fitted at the base of its stem. It was a float I'd used for many years and which brought me a great deal of success. It was not, however, all that easy to use, the most difficult trick, if you can call it that, being to maintain a satisfactory tautness of the line between rod tip and the base of the float. Correspondence over the years since the first edition of this book appeared merely emphasised that many anglers had problems in this direction.

These days, however, the Ducker, though it will still perform as well as ever if properly used, is little used. Many are the alternatives employed in its stead, the most common word used to describe them being Wagglers.

As a point of passing interest, this name, I understand, was first bestowed on this type of float by anglers in the North West when, in the early seventies, they were experimenting with straight peacock quill floats fished bottom only. That well-known North Western wit, Richard Bowker, senior, of Leigh in Lancashire, making his first tentative casts with the float, watched its flight with no little interest and announced: "It just goes wagglety-wagglety." I understand it was a matter of hours before the name waggler was bestowed.

While I have mixed feelings about some of the alternatives which have emerged to the Ducker, there is not the slightest doubt these floats, in all their forms, are extremely popular indeed and are widely and successfully used by thousands of anglers.

Even more important, and this is worth emphasis at the outset, is that all these floats (like the Ducker before them) not only enable one to beat the downstream wind condition on a river, they are also first class when it comes to fishing still water. This means that unless a shotting diagram makes this clear later in the chapter you can presume we are talking about a float that will perform in both settings.

Before I discuss the Ducker alternatives, I think it important to begin with the Ducker itself for it is still used and some, I know, still prefer it. It's also useful for it gives me an early opportunity to show how shotting patterns may be changed to cope with a) the downstream wind on a river and b) the still water situation.

To look at, the Ducker is for all the world like an upside down Avon float. Mine have a cane stem and a balsa wood body near the base which is not loaded, this latter being a

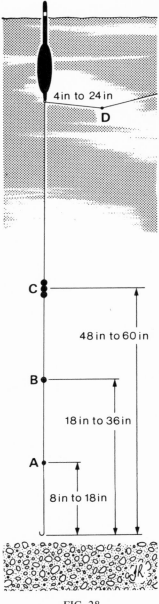

FIG. 28

consideration I'll be referring to again later in this chapter.

For river fishing in a downstreamer with the Ducker, I prefer a shotting pattern (Fig. 28) which is a simplification of those shown in earlier editions of this book. The tell-tale (shot A) alternates its position for reasons with which, by now, you should be totally familiar, the strength of bites. B is a stabilising shot which also helps to guard against the fairly remote possibility with this float of back tangles. C are the bulk shot designed to speed the tackle down through the water so that the earliest possible indication is obtained, this being especially useful if a fish intercepts the bait during its fall. The back shot (D) is there to beat the wind and drag. The stronger either or both are, the further this shot should be placed from the base of the float, up to the maximum of 24 inches as shown. When fishing, you now try to maintain a reasonably tight line from rod to tip to this back shot. As I have hinted earlier, it can be tricky but any difficulty should be overcome with practice. The float, incidentally, is fixed to the line by a series of loops through the eyelet ring as described earlier.

The two most important things to remember when fishing a Ducker in a river are a) always try and maintain a reasonably tight line between rod tip and back shot and b) never check the float or your return will be a false bite.

Consider now the use of the Ducker in still water (Fig. 29). As you can see, the shotting pattern is not dissimilar to that in Fig. 28, being, in fact, simply a scaled down version of it. The tactic with this rig is to cast beyond the baited area and then, by turning the reel with the rod tip submerged, draw the tackle back to the desired spot, a movement which will ensure not only a tight line between rod and float but also that the line is submerged below the surface away from the wind and drag.

Let's move on now to the various alternatives which have emerged in recent years for the Duckers.

And first there's what most call the Straight Waggler. This is simply a straight piece of peacock quill fitted with a float ring at its base. The advantage claimed for this quill

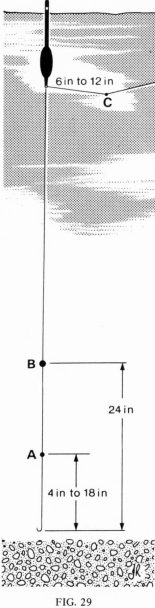

FIG. 29

as a material is the perfectly correct one that, as it is so buoyant, it is capable of carrying more shot, thus improving the casting range. Its main disadvantage, in my view, is that anglers using these floats tend to fish much heavier than is really necessary.

Another error they make (and this applies to almost all the floats in the Waggler family) is that instead of fishing the float attached to the line with a series of loops through the bottom ring, they stop the float in position on the line with a shot either side of the ring; this is known as the locked shot system (see Fig. 16). By fixing the float in this way (and I know many will disagree with me), you are destroying some of its buoyancy. Add the fact that, most often, it's the shot used in this position that are heavier than necessary and I maintain that this overloading also interferes with the float's stability. Third and, perhaps, most important, it is my opinion that locked shot can interfere with the speed of the strike. When the strike is made the object is to eliminate the angle between rod, float and hook as quickly as possible. Those locking shots, in my view, can mean that this movement is delayed, albeit only momentarily. That delay, however, can often add up to the difference between a well set hook and a missed fish.

So if you want to use these floats, take my tip—fix them with line loops. I realise this works against the kind of quick float changing offered by certain line fixtures which are on the market these days but, at least, you can feel you are fishing the rig in its most efficient form.

Let's look now at the question of fishing a Straight Waggler in a downstream wind. When roach are the fish being caught and especially when caster is the hookbait, I prefer a pattern which might best be described as a variation between the famous string-of-shot system and the Avon pattern. Look now at the diagram (Fig. 30). The float is fixed by loops through the ring and the bulk shot (A) are placed some four inches below it. Between this point and the tell-tale (B) all the remaining shots are spaced evenly.

Where the hovering effect for the bait produced by

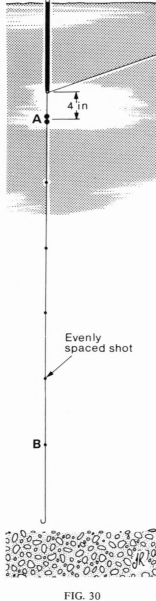

4 in

A

Evenly
spaced shot

B

FIG. 30

checking the string system is not required, the float can be shotted to the same pattern as Fig. 29 but *without* the back shot.

Yet another alternative with this float (and it is useful) is to use what is called a Spliced Waggler. This is simply a piece of peacock with a second, thinner piece spliced into the top to give a thinner tip or antenna to the float. This is specially helpful when the fish are biting shyly, the thinner tip being easier to submerge. Shotting patterns remain unchanged.

Next in this family comes the bodied Waggler. This is simply a piece of straight peacock quill with a body (usually made of balsa) fitted near the base like the Ducker. Known to some as the Swinger, the basic object of this float is to increase the distance that may be cast and to increase the speed of the bait's descent in the water, both of these being achieved because of the greater shot carrying capacity offered by the addition to the body of the float. Though I know these floats are widely used, I favour another alternative of the same pattern which I'll discuss in a moment. Suffice it to say for the meantime that this float can be fished with the shotting patterns shown in Figs. 28, 29 and 30.

So much, then, for the first of our alternatives to the Ducker, a float which, like so many others, I must confess I have stopped using. If, meanwhile, I have seemed less enthusiastic about these Waggler patterns which, it's got to be admitted, are widely used, that's simply because I prefer something else . . . especially when the problem is beating a downstream wind on a river. Whether you'll share my enthusiasm for this further alternative is entirely up to you. All I can say is that it works for me and I hope after reading what I've got to say about it you'll come to feel that the same could be true for you. It is, in fact, a float I referred to earlier in this book, the Mini-Missile. Having already extolled its virtues in the still water setting, let us now consider its advantages in the downstream wind situation. The float, as you will recall, has a peacock quill stem with a balsa body looking to all the world like the bodied Waggler we've just been discussing. The main difference, and it's an important one, is that the Mini-Missile has a loading in the shape of a piece of brass rod in its base. What, you are bound to ask immediately, are the advantages?

There are several. The first, already made clear earlier, is that because the float is loaded you can cover even greater casting ranges and, just as important, you can do so with a minimum amount of shot down the line. To give a simple example as we are, after all, talking about alternatives to the Ducker, the biggest Ducker specified in earlier editions of this book took the equivalent of four swan shot. The biggest Mini-Missile I need takes a maximum of three AAAs. The loading in the float gives the float extra stability (remember this when you're considering the use of locked shots) and it also makes for a smooth, direct trajectory on the cast. It retains one disadvantage common to all bottom only floats in a downstreamer: it cannot be checked without producing a false bite. On the other hand, it is much easier to retain a reasonably tight line to the float than it was to, say, the Ducker simply because it is more stable.

I offer two shotting patterns for the Mini-Missile in this setting. The first (Fig. 31) is what I call my general bait pattern, this being the one used when using such offerings as maggot, worm or bread. The float is fixed to the line by the float ring *never* with locked shots. Shot A is the tell-tale which, in this instance, alternates in two ways, its distance from the hook and its size. The question of distance is governed by the factor I've mentioned so often before, the strength of the bites. The size of the tell-tale shot varies for two reasons. The bigger the bait (i.e. worm as opposed to maggot) the bigger this shot should be within the limitations shown and the stronger the flow again the bigger it should be. The bulk shot (B) are all pinched on together 18 inches above A, this being to ensure the tackle is fishing efficiently as soon as possible after it enters the water. Unlike the Ducker, the Mini-Missile requires no back shot because of its body loading and because it's longer than a Ducker; this latter facility also making it easier to bury the line. Without

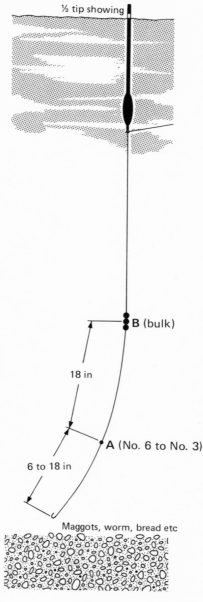

FIG. 31

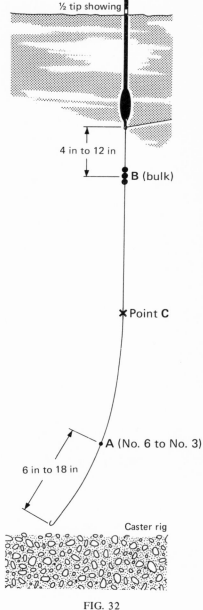

½ tip showing

4 in to 12 in

B (bulk)

✗ Point C

● A (No. 6 to No. 3)

6 in to 18 in

Caster rig

FIG. 32

doubt, there's an overall improvement in tackle control with this float.

The second rig (Fig. 32) is specially designed for fishing the caster, particularly in waters where the temperatures vary in such a way that fish are moved to feed at varying levels. The aim of this pattern is to enable you to present the bait at the required level. This is not done by checking the float. That, as I have already said, would simply lead to a false submersion. With this rig, I'm capitalising on the braking effect provided by the marginal water which always runs slower than that further out into the stream. Shot A is again an alternator for more than the usual reason. Apart from the question of bites, this varies in size on the basis of the flow, the stronger it is the larger of the shots specified is used. The placing of the bulk shot (B) is specially important. The depth is the important factor here. If the water is between 3 and 4 feet deep, these shot would be set 4 inches below the float. The deeper the water (and I'm thinking of a maximum for comfortable fishing of 8 feet) the further down the line from the float these shot go until they reach the maximum distance specified of 12 inches. The relevance of point C? This, as you can see, is the midway point between B and A. I mark it for this reason. When you are fishing a depth beyond 4 feet, I find it best to remove one of the bulk shot (most often a BB) and place this at point C. This, I find, helps the tackle continue to give the correct movement to the caster, the kind of up and down shift which fish seem to find tantalising. Still on caster, in winter, when the water temperature is not varying in the way I have described, I tend to fish the caster to the pattern shown in Fig. 31.

There remains one other circumstance to be covered when the wind is downstream on a river—what to do when the water is deeper than your rod? The answer—and it should be no surprise—is to use a sliding float and the one I favour in this situation is the sliding Peacock Antenna, first described in a still water setting in Chapter 4. The shotting pattern to employ is the same as that shown earlier (see

Fig. 14). It's worth adding that while this float is basically designed for water deeper than the rod, it's often more comfortable to use a slider at more modest depths, say from 8 feet upwards, this being especially true when the bank behind you is high and there is some obstruction present, like a bush, which could impede casting.

8 The Trent Trotter

Many of the great breakthroughs in angling techniques have been made by chance. And none came more by chance than the float I want to tell you about now—a float which gave me a bigger thrill in its invention than any other—the Trent Trotter. It's an odd, unlikely looking thing, I'll readily admit. But in certain circumstances no other piece of tackle could possibly achieve what this float can.

In a nutshell, it's a float for long-trotting extremely shallow swims—and by shallow I mean as little as 6 inches—at long distances.

I think the best way of helping you understand this little angler's 'must' is by telling you the story of how I came to develop it. And how, finally, a series of accidents occurred which made it more complete than even I had thought possible.

The story began some years ago when I was taking part in the Trent Championship. I had had a bad draw and was placed five pegs below Gunthorpe Weir where the water was extremely shallow as far out as anyone could reasonably throw.

I used a centre-pin reel and although I reckon I can cast as far as any man with one of these, even the mightiest heave was only taking me out to water 12 inches deep at the most.

My only answer in the float department was my regular stand-by, an Avon—which then had a longish crowquill stem and a round cork body about an inch from the tip. I had to use a big one, about 9 inches long, to get my bait out. In water only a foot deep, you can imagine how that cramped my style.

By putting a long tail under the float I was just about able to manage and I started to get a few fish. But I suffered badly from the hazard all anglers meet in shallow water like this, back tangles. If I had one, I had dozens—but I remained convinced that this method was the only one on this day which was going to get me any fish.

Then something happened which gave me the first clue on the route that led me finally to the Trent Trotter. I snapped the float stem just below the cork when striking at a fish. That left just a broken stub, the cork and the tip.

Time was running out, so I decided it was too late to change floats. I merely fixed the remains of my Avon back on the line with a valve rubber on the tip and another on the broken stem. I cast in and, to my surprise, began getting much clearer bite indication and more fish. I still suffered the occasional tangle, but it was obviously a great improvement.

At the end of the match I had 7 pounds 12 ounces, a catch which won me the Trentman badge for one of the best weights in my zone. I was surprised and delighted and even more determined to master the frustration I'd suffered from this shallow Trent swim. For after all, there were plenty more like it and I might easily draw another the next time.

I realised—it's obvious now!—that my first little accident had permitted me one important advantage. The loss of that long float stem gave me greater leeway at the tail end. This was sufficient for me to use a terminal shot which was far more likely to keep my hook out of the way of the float on the long cast.

Clearly, if I had been able to fish just the Avon's cork body and tip, while still being able to attach it top and bottom, things would have been even better. But that just wasn't possible.

Later, at home, I bore this in mind when I produced my first prototype of the Trotter. The float itself has changed little since that first pattern and is basically an Avon with no stem, except that it has a pear-shaped rather than a round cork body.

But that wasn't all that needed solving. The shotting pattern was something which foxed me for months and finally was only resolved by two more even happier accidents than the first. Even now when I think of how they happened I can't stop a smile . . . and a very self-satisfied one at that, I don't mind admitting.

When I first tried out the prototype there was a shot above the float to help me bury the line. But it was fairly close, about 12 inches. All I had beneath the float was one AAA, 1 inch below it, a BB a little farther down, and a No. 1 shot 6 inches from the hook.

The rig worked like this, but only up to a point. The big disadvantage was that on the strike the float offered such resistance that any fish I hit were literally hurtled to the surface, causing just the kind of shoal-disturbing splash I was most anxious to avoid in such shallow water.

Time and again, these turbulent strikes sent the shoals away. Nevertheless, I was sure I was catching more fish this way than I would have done with an orthodox float of the Avon type.

Then came the second accident. I was pleasure fishing with the float when I got a tangle which led to the line between rod and float, and the line between the float and the first shot down the line, being held firmly together.

As I was not in a match, and the tangle was a real corker, I carelessly cast in again without making any real attempt to undo it. Within a few minutes I had another bite, but this time the fish wasn't rushed to the surface. Instead I was able to get it out without causing the slightest disturbance to the shoal.

I sat down on my basket for a quiet ponder and after a few minutes realisation dawned. That first shot under the float, because it was gripping the line between rod and float *and* the line between fish and float, was acting like a pendulum. This put me in contact with the fish more quickly and—more important still—reduced the resistance caused by the float on the strike.

I quickly re-set the tackle, pinching both lines cleanly into that first shot. As more fish came to the net I soon found that everytime I struck, the float promptly went straight under and stayed there until I had played the fish well away from the shoal.

But there came a third accident. Although I don't see it as being as important as the first two, it still gave me one of the biggest angling thrills of my life. For it happened on no less an occasion than the National Championship.

It was in the 1961 National in the Trent when, as you must have guessed, I drew one of the shallowest swims in the river. I didn't win but I came near enough in this apparently impossible swim to make me as happy as I've ever been.

When I got to my peg for this match, my heart sank. It was far, far worse than I had expected. I was drawn just above Stoke weir in one of the shallowest reaches of the river. Thirty yards out from the bank it was only a foot deep!

My usual gallery was already waiting for me as I began to tackle up. They seemed to sense it was a tough old swim and one wag called out to me: 'We'll see how good you are today.'

Fortunately, I did have the Trent Trotter and, while I never expected to win a match in the swim, I knew my little float gave me a chance of saving my face at the least.

Little did I realise how much more than that it was going to do for me. The third in a series of accidents with this float was going to happen, in the most important match there is, giving me the last clue to the final shotting pattern you see illustrated here (Fig. 33). But I'm racing ahead.

The wind on this day was distinctly nasty . . . downstream and across. It seemed to get stronger as the minutes ticked away to the start of the match. There were titters from behind which I could only take for indications that some of my spectators were really looking forward to seeing me struggle.

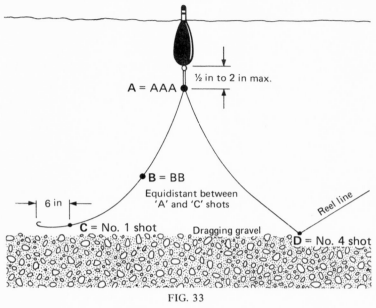

½ in to 2 in max.

A = AAA

B = BB
Equidistant between
'A' and 'C' shots

6 in

C = No. 1 shot

Dragging gravel

Reel line

D = No. 4 shot

FIG. 33

I used the Trotter from the start and there were one or two sniggers when I produced it for the first time. Maybe it was because it does look a bit like a pilot float for pike that one onlooker was inspired to remark: 'Blimey! He's going pike fishing.'

There were other discomforts at the start of this day. And they got worse. My basket had to rest in six inches of water and every time the lock gates opened I had to move farther out into the river. In one instance I moved out twelve yards.

Once we were 'off' I cheered up for, sure enough, I started getting some fish with the Trotter. I had taken about 4 pound when it became obvious that the fish in my keepnet were in extreme discomfort because of the shallowness of the water.

I called for the steward who weighed the fish before releasing them. Then, as I had to move forward yet again, the steward dug a hole in the shingle for my keep-net so that there would be water deep enough to hold any fish which followed without damage.

Naturally, all this performing was doing great things for my morale!

But I got stuck in once more and again began catching small fish regularly. At the same time, the wind was slowly, but surely, getting worse making fishing more and more difficult. To give you some idea of how seriously I took it, it's the only match on the Trent I have ever fished with a fixed-spool reel—because of the enormous casts I had to make to get out to the fish.

Because of the worsening wind I moved shot D (see Fig. 33) some four feet away from the float. My only aim was, as before, to sink the line—but quicker.

This turned out to be lucky accident number three with this float. For what happened? I found that I had now got this shot so far from the float it was dragging on the shingle behind the float as I trotted down and—most important of all—was acting like a brake on the tackle.

Just like that it gave me complete control of the tackle in conditions which should have made a mockery of any attempt to fish in them! My only worry was that with this shot so low in the water it would impede the strike. But this did not turn out to be the case. In water this shallow it simply made no difference.

I started to take fish rapidly then but, as so often happens on the Trent, a barge ploughed through and dispersed the shoal. Determined not to be beaten, I immediately began feeding again and twenty minutes later once more started catching roach.

Now I was getting a fish a throw. It seemed unbelievable. At the end I had 17 pounds 4 ounces and that made me fourth individual in the match—a position not one of those people watching, nor even I, would have believed possible at the start.

While my World Championship win and my third in the 1956 Witham National had pleased me greatly, I don't think there was ever a day's fishing in which I felt happier about problems solved than this one. I couldn't stop thinking about that little shot, how I had moved it, and what a tremendous difference it had made to everything. There were so many others in much, much better swims who could have beaten me and I'd beaten them, in what looked the most diabolical piece of water on the entire river.

There were no titters at the end of this match—just the odd gaping mouth here and there. But best of all was the thrill I got the following year when the National Federation of Anglers' annual conference was held in Coventry. Two Nottingham delegates, who had watched me all those months before, came round specially to see me to tell me they would never forget the way in which I had beaten this swim. It was a touching moment.

Having told you the story of how my Trent Trotter came into being I hope I have helped you grasp more easily how it works.

Just to make certain, let's have a little re-cap with the diagram (Fig. 33 again). The first important shot is A. This is the one in which you pinch the line from the reel *and* the line going down to the hook, the shot which gives the tackle that vital pendulum quality which prevents extreme disturbance in the sort of shallow water where the float will be used.

You can see I've made it an alternator and its final position depends on the depth of the swim. The most water you would fish with this rig would be 2 feet deep, the least 6 inches. The rule of thumb is that shot A is farthest from the float in the deepest water.

The setting of shots B and C is again determined largely by the prevailing depth. In the diagram the setting is for a swim 2 feet deep and bear in mind, too, that you fish over depth. In other words, the distance from the float to the hook in these conditions would be 2 feet 6 inches.

In shallower places—say one foot and less—shot B would be moved up to join shot A and, like shot A, would be pinched on to both lines to add to the pendulum effect.

Shot C in 2 feet of water would be as shown in the diagram. At lower levels, it would be not less than 4 inches.

You have got to use your own discretion to some extent

about the length of tail you fish with this rig. If, for instance, you were fishing with flake for chub in 6 inches of water you would have a long tail of, say, 2 feet. But if on the other hand, you were maggot fishing you should keep the tail as short as possible.

Shot D's position can only be judged when you actually begin fishing. The strength of the flow can affect its place for, while you want it to drag the bottom behind the tackle, you want it *only just* dragging and not hard on.

The only yardstick I can offer for this—and it is a real generalisation—is that the distance of shot D above the float is usually exactly twice the depth of the water.

Once you have got the rig set, it is the easiest in the world to fish with. You can cast overhand or underhand. Tangles should be non-existent. Bites will be shown by a crystal clear submerging of the float tip.

Only one thing needs watching after you've started—the speed of the water. If it's very fast you might well find that a heavier shot at point D is needed to give you the right braking effect. But that's the only change you are likely to need.

Now I said when we first began discussing the Trotter that it looks a bit outlandish. But, believe me, it isn't. There is no other tackle which will take fish from shallow running water to come within miles of it . . . as I hope the discoveries I've told you about will have proved.

One last word for do-it-yourself float makers. The float is 2 inches long from tip to base and the body is a pear-shaped cork or piece of balsa ½ inch at its widest. The tip is cane fitted into the top of the cork. When you've fixed these together all that needs to be added is the float ring at the base.

9 The Trout Trotter

The Trout Trotter is another of my own inventions—wrongly named, perhaps, for I also use it for chub.

Basically, it's a variation of the small pilot float pike fishers sometimes use. Its purpose is to permit easy fishing in fast, shallow water—especially the kind that contains plenty of obstructions and weed clumps, swims, in other words, that most would be inclined to reject as impossible for float fishing, even with the float we've just discussed, the Trent Trotter.

When using the Trout Trotter I am, almost without exception, after trout. A live minnow works a treat with it on jungly waters like the Windrush, the Evenlode and, until they banned floats during the close season for coarse fish, on the Wye and on the Severn.

Exempted from this are the Windrush chub. For I use this float for them, too, but with flake instead of minnow.

If you don't fish the waters I have mentioned there may be waters like them in your area so, first, I think it best if I tell you more in detail about the kind of conditions this float is out to beat.

The Windrush is a small but rugged river where the depth is rarely greater than two feet, much of it completely broken water rushing forcefully between boulders and thick weed clumps. In places, it's even weedier than the Hampshire Avon—a veritable jungle in fact.

The Evenlode, it must be admitted, is more placid having plenty of sluggish glides. But here, too, there's broken water and, in places, the most prolific weed growth.

On both these rivers, the only bait I use with this float when fishing for trout is live minnow and, having said that, I'm sure you will now see that the entire rig could best be described as a miniature pike set-up.

For many years I accepted the pilot float—it's like a small *Fishing Gazette* float—as standard for this kind of water. But, as I tried to explain with the Trent Trotter, I found that by attaching the float at the bottom only instead of having it run through the central bore of the float I fished more lightly, more smoothly, and, more important still, disturbed the swim less when striking at a taking fish.

At the same time, you must appreciate that it is a float designed for the shallowest of waters—say between 6 inches and 2 feet. Why not, you might ask, merely use the Trent Trotter? The answer is (a) because it is not necessary and (b) because the more complicated shotting of that float is specifically designed for long distance work.

The Trout Trotter is a much simpler job for fishing at much closer quarters.

It is the simplest of rigs (Fig. 34). Look first at shot C. Its placing is not really tied up at all with the buoyancy of the tackle. It is where it is to keep the minnow well down in the water. And its distance from the hook is determined by the depth of the water and the strength of its flow.

Bear in mind, too, that the tackle is always fished over depth, i.e. in 2 feet of water there'd be a 3 feet trace below the float. In really rugged shallow water, shot C would be only 6 inches from the hook.

To try and make this aspect of the thing clearer: I should never have a trace below the float of less than 2 feet and if I was reduced to this the water I should be fishing would be only 6 inches deep. It follows, I hope, that in 2 feet of water, the cast below the float would be at least 4 feet.

Shots A and B are lumped together just under the float for two reasons . . . to give you weight for casting and to help the float hold up well in rough conditions.

With this rig, you do not keep a tight line from float to rod tip although you do aim to keep in reasonable touch.

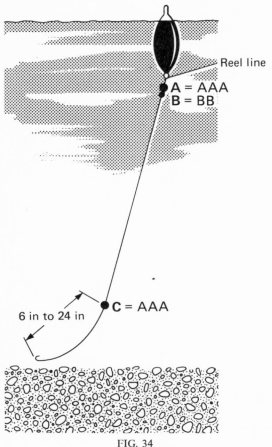

Reel line

A = AAA
B = BB

C = AAA

6 in to 24 in

FIG. 34

The main thing is ensure that the minnow is able to work freely.

It's mostly in winter when I get round to using this float for chub. The shotting arrangement doesn't change and while there's still plenty of foliage about you should find, with a sufficiently large piece of flake coupled with that AAA downstairs, it should pull its own way easily through even the thickest of clumps. If you used heavier terminal leads you would have great difficulty guiding the tackle along in this way.

It might be interesting for you to know why I came to

126

reject the ordinary pilot float. First of all, they are generally far too gaudy for working in small waters. The Trout Trotter is dark green with a black tip.

Second, and more important, one found that with the pilot float when working a minnow a fair distance down a small brook some of the line between rod and float would be submerged. The trouble with this being that you never got a really clean strike. With the Trotter this fault is virtually eliminated and the line doesn't wander nearly so much because the float is fastened at the bottom only.

Another point well worth considering is that with a natural minnow a certain amount of control is needed over the bait—but not too much. With some floats the minnow would wander all over the place. But with the Trotter you get just the right kind of control. It roams—but not too far and not too eratically.

Like the Trent Trotter and the Zoomer, the Trout Trotter is limited in its uses but it's well worth having a couple in your float box for the right occasion.

In fact, it's this kind of comprehensiveness in your float box that I've been trying to aim at all along. Complete the selection I am giving you and there's no water anywhere— given various sizes of each float—that you will not be able to beat.

10 Pole Float Basics

Though I have never indulged to any serious extent in pole fishing, mostly because, latterly, I have largely ceased to fish matches for health reasons, I like to think this is a subject on which I can offer some initial guidance not least because I think I can take some credit for the pole fishing craze which has swept the British match fishing scene since the early seventies.

In the sixties, poles were largely unknown in Britain. As always, we mostly used the rod and running line approach which has been traditional with us for so long and which, I still maintain, remains the most satisfying way of catching fish, quite apart from being the most efficient when bigger fish are the quarry.

When I won the World Championship in 1963, I did so using running line tackle with a centre pin reel though my Continental opponents on that occasion fished the pole the way they have always done. At that match, I became friendly with the great French angler Robert Tesse, for many years the captain of their team and still the only man ever to win the individual title in the World event three times.

Later, and I've now reached the early seventies, *Angler's Mail*, the national angling paper to which I was then contributing a weekly column, decided it would be an interesting idea to set up a meeting in France at which I would meet Robert and we would fish and discuss our two contrasting approaches in tackle in the hope that the result would be of interest to our readers. If the comments I received at the time were anything to go by, I'm sure we succeeded. Here were born the first feelings that the pole approach might have something to offer English match anglers, the interest at first being keenest in the North West where, like the French, many anglers had long favoured the bloodworm as a hook bait.

Not long after this, it was decided that it would be interesting to carry this discussion further by staging friendly matches between France and England, the venue varying from country to country each year. It would be fair to say that once these matches began to be fished in this country, where English anglers could see at first hand how the French pole anglers operated, the likely conversion of many match anglers to the pole began to snowball.

About this same time, the National Federation of Anglers, the body responsible for recruiting England's World Championship team, took the progressive step of abandoning their existing system of selecting their squad. Until this time, it had consisted of one angler from each of the teams that finished in the top six in the previous year's National Championship, a situation which meant that the team was literally being picked by six local angling associations. Though I gained entry to the team myself by this system, I never considered it the best method. And so the Federation changed things, by appointing a team manager who turned out to be my old friend and Coventry team-mate, Stan Smith, with a selection committee. Later still, Stan was given complete control over the selection, in my view the best method of all. As a result of this change, interest in England's fortunes in the event increased out of all recognition and, when it became apparent that the very best we could field was still being beaten by Continental pole anglers, interest in pole fishing escalated still further until today we find that a pole is a normal part of the equipment of every thinking match angler.

It is not my intention here to produce a full scale dissertation on the methods of pole fishing. Such an object would demand a book in itself. What I do want to do, however, is talk about floats, for in this department, as in so many others relating to float fishing, patterns are being offered which are nothing like so useful as their inventors would have us believe.

With so many anglers here still at what might be called a beginner's stage with the pole, I want to recommend them, at least at the outset, to stick to what might be called the basic pattern for this kind of fishing. Indeed, I'd say the float I'm going to talk about should be good for almost all eventualities. I know Robert Tesse used no other up to the time I met him and his record surely speaks for itself.

The float in question (see Fig. 35) is simply a slender piece of balsa with a bristle fitted into the top as an antenna. It is fixed to the line by passing the latter first through a small eyelet ring fixed to the side of the float near the top and out through a piece of plastic tubing at the base. This fixture, while it locks the float safely in position, is still not so tight that the float cannot be moved easily up and down the line to cater for changes in depth. Usually, the body of the float is painted black. The collar at the top of the body and the antenna are painted white and when the float is fished only the antenna or antenna and collar is visible.

The important thing about the use of the pole with this float is the positiveness of the presentation of the bait to the fish and that of the strike.

The standard pattern used by the French to fish this float couldn't be simpler (see Fig. 36). Most of the weight used to cock the float is in the form of an Olivette. This is a pear-shaped lead (sold in various weights) with a hole through the centre. The lead is threaded on the line and stopped from running down to the hook by a shot. Care must be taken to make sure the lead is an exact match for the float so that the latter is correctly 'dotted' when being fished.

The best way to achieve this is to test the loading in a bucket or in the bath. Indeed, this pre-testing points to one of the other advantages of pole fishing, the way in which the entire tackle, float, weights, and hook are made up together before fishing and stored on a winder. On the bank, all you have to do is attach the end of the line to your pole, undo the winder, and you are in business. It follows that the pole angler who means to succeed will have a wide variety of tackles made up in this way, permitting him to fish the same rig at various depths with different line strengths and different sizes of hook, each one, of course, ready for use at a moment's notice with the quick change system offered by the pole system.

But let's get back to our basic float. Once the right Olivette

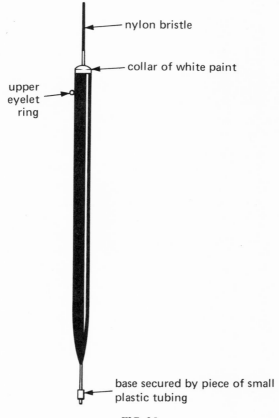

FIG. 35

has been found to balance the float, the main question is where to put it on the line. There have been plenty of fancy ideas suggested but I know Robert Tesse invariably went for something like the rig in our diagram. If you are going to fish a swim that is say between 7 and 8 feet deep which is still or sluggish, the Olivette should be placed exactly 2 feet from the hook with tackle set so that the hook but *not* the weight is just on the bottom. Six inches from the hook goes your tell-tale. It couldn't be simpler.

This rig is for conditions which may be considered normal but what if, as can happen in a river setting, the flow is too strong for the rig described? The answer is to move the Olivette nearer the hook. Just how much depends on trial and error. If bites are being satisfactorily hit in the changed setting, you know you've got it right. Sometimes, it may be necessary to move the Olivette down until it is just 6 inches from the hook and the tell-tale has been dispensed with. That may seem a strange thing to anglers who have long felt that lightness at the business end of their tackle was essential but, believe me, when the flow really does develop this is needed.

Indeed, one of the most important things with this rig is to constantly think about the position of the Olivette in relationship to the regularity of the bites you are getting. When bites slow, the invariable answer in flowing water is to move the Olivette nearer to the hook.

In deeper water where you want the bait to get down quickly to the fish, you should still start with the Olivette 2 feet from the hook with a tell-tale though to achieve the quick drop you'd switch to a bigger float coupled with a bigger Olivette.

As the tip of the pole is being fished directly over the float this gives a much more positive strike than is possible with rod and running line when, usually, much line has to be picked on the strike before the fish is hooked.

Look now at Fig. 36 and the way the line is passed through the upper ring first. This method of fitting offers another advantage—it allows the float to be held back

Line fixed at
top through
upper ring

Olivette

stop shot

24 in

6 in

FIG. 36

without causing the float itself to lift in the water. The teasing effect the French give to their hook baits holding back in this way is something you should aim to produce, too, for it often results in a bite when a static bait or, in rivers, one fished with the speed of flow, just does not produce.

As I am sure you would agree, the set-up is simplicity itself, one of the simplest, in fact, in this entire book. This is why it's so positive.

One other tip when setting up this tackle is to ensure that the distance between the float and the pole tip is not too great, say 6 feet at most but, preferably 3 or 4. The mistake so many pole fishing beginners make is to cast the float out beyond the pole tip when, in fact, you should always aim to fish with the pole tip as near as possible directly over the top of the float, this position ensuring that you get the most positive strike. To fish with the float beyond the pole (as one so often does with running line tackle) is simply to lose one of the greatest single advantages offered by a pole in the first place, the more direct strike.

As I said at the outset, this is a very basic look at pole fishing, my only concern being to get you started with the right kind of float. There are other floats and tackles, most of them aimed at catching smaller fish (like bleak) but these are something you should think of graduating to later after accustoming yourself to the pole fishing style with the rig I've shown. Start with the ideas I have given here—they have after all, come from one of the most impeccable sources there is—and you will find your entry into the world of pole fishing much easier and more logical than might otherwise have been the case.

Conclusion

One of the keenest discussions you are ever likely to hear when anglers are talking about floats is the old and still vexed question as to what colour they should be. It has been said that the majority of floats in most tackle shops are there to catch anglers and not fish. While this is still true to some extent, the general quality of floats offered for sale today is infinitely better than it was a few years ago and it's still improving.

My own feeling on this question of colour is that the best colour for the body of a float is dark green closely followed by dark brown. These are my personal choices but I would accept any argument favouring any dark colour which could be presumed to offer camouflage.

The finish should most definitely be dull. They may look nicer with a shiny bright varnish on them but not for me. The tip here is to use a dull varnish.

The question of colour for the tip of a float is something else again for this is a factor which depends a great deal on light conditions on the day. If there is a ripple and a shine on the water—especially from the sun—then black for me is the only colour for the tip. If the day is dull and the water comparatively free of ripples then white would be my choice. When conditions are not rough and the sun is behind me then orange or yellow would be my selection.

I am also a great believer in two-colour tips. While my feeling about the extreme end of the tip is unvarying, I also like a second band of colour beneath this one running down below the float's waterline. With a black tip, this band would be white, and with white, orange or yellow tips it would be black.

As I see it, if you have about 1 inch of tip showing and it's of the same colour, a slight lift bite could easily be missed, especially if you are fishing any distance out from the bank. If, on the other hand, you have a two-colour tip that little lift will most often lead to the uncovering of that second colour and then you are in no doubt about what is happening.

Now while my basic tastes are for black or white tips I wouldn't like to be too dogmatic about it because this may be because my eyes may be more sensitive to these colours than anyone else's.

Make sure every float you own is completely watertight. There is nothing more annoying than to discover after half-an-hour's fishing that your float is waterlogged and sinking all the time as a result. Quill floats are most prone to leak and should be checked regularly for holes, remembering that even the smallest pin prick is enough to spoil them.

Now, in conclusion, I would like to justify my choice of floats in terms of angling logic. Every float dealt with in the preceding chapters was presented for a reason and, now you have read this far, I hope you will have realised why the order in which they were discussed was so deliberate.

My aim was to start at the simplest point moving forward as each new problem called for a new outlook and I think a quick recapitulation is needed here to help you finally get the floats in perspective for if you can understand clearly why I placed them in the order I did, I am sure you will eventually come to select the right float for the right occasion almost by instinct.

The first float we dealt with was the simple Crowquill, a float which may still be considered the basis from which many other developments have stemmed. Presented with ideal conditions, the Crowquill will still cope with them as well as ever it did. These days, however, Crowquills, sadly, are not as readily available as they were. To bridge this gap, I offered you an alternative float, the Canal Antenna.

Unfortunately, conditions are not always as benign as these floats demand and so we learnt the first main lesson about any kind of float fishing. The conditions always dictate the pattern that must be used, the most important factor of all being the wind.

Indeed, we found that the main thing that prevented us using these ideal floats was wind (though perhaps breeze would be a better word in this instance) for we found that it meant we could no longer present the bait in the place we wanted.

We got round this in the still water setting I considered first by switching to other things. Our first main alternative was the Dart, the alternative to the Reverse Crowquill and the first of a number of floats which allowed us the most important advantage of being able to sink the line out of the way of the wind.

But all winds are not breezes and, pretty soon, we discovered that even these floats, while they did permit the line to be buried, eventually turned out to be too light to permit casting accurately to the chosen spot.

The answer was to scale up through floats like the Onion, the first float to be mentioned of that typical pattern which has a body attached to the base of the stem. It's worth recalling the reasons for this for they are basic to all floats of this type. It gave the float greater buoyancy thus allowing it to hold up better in rougher conditions. Equally important, it allowed for a greater shot load thus enabling you to bridge the casting gap.

Later, we considered floats for fishing this kind of water at long range, when the swim to be fished was deeper than the length of the rod, and a combination of the two.

Next and still, I hope, in a logical sequence, we considered the problems offered by river fishing, especially, again, the vital effects of the wind.

We tackled first the easiest condition to cope with, the upstream wind, considering various patterns fixed top and bottom which allowed one to deal with almost every eventuality in this circumstance.

The next and more difficult problem was how to float fish rivers in a downstream wind. In earlier editions of this book, the time honoured Ducker float was our main weapon but, as I showed, this has now been replaced by a whole range of floats offering a variety of answers to this important problem. Remember, too, that many of these had an equally useful function in still water simply because they were all floats that were fixed bottom only.

On, then, to the problem of long range river fishing in extremely shallow water solved by the use of the Trent Trotter.

Finally, I offered some basic advice for the many who are now taking up pole fishing for the first time. The float I suggested was basic and, at this moment in time, I cannot believe that anything like the number of alternatives will emerge for use with this system as we have found with the running line. The pole method is too obvious and direct to permit too much variation.

Looking back over the sequence, you may still feel a little confused as to just which float is the right one to use. The answer is to ask yourself a series of questions when faced with your chosen swim. What is the wind doing? What sort of water have I got? Is it still, flowing, shallow, deep, fast, or slow? How turbulent is it? Is it weedy or obstructed? What kind of fish are likely to be encountered: bottom, surface or mid-water feeders? Whatever the answers, I'm certain you'll find that one of the floats you have just been reading about will fill the bill.

Finally, I would like to give you a few golden rules for float fishing which have served me in good stead over the years.

And first is the question of materials. In certain chapters I tried to persuade you that some were better for making floats than others.

All quills used for making floats should be as straight as possible and free of leaks. For float bodies, cork used to be the most favoured material, and it's still good. On the other hand, it would be true to say that balsa is much more often used these days and, for most, seems just as satisfactory.

Now in use many floats are abused and I have lost count of the number of times I have walked along riversides only to see perfectly good floats being fished wrongly.

Often it's a case of men using a huge float which is three times larger than the job calls for. The tip here: always use the lightest tackle permitted by the conditions.

Still more will have great chunks of floats sticking out of the water—so large no fish could pull it under.

The tip: always make sure that the 'show' on your float is the minimum possible compatible with accurate bite detection.

Shotting is another problem which seems to perplex too many. But it would be no problem at all if only these people would realise that the simple answer is to arm yourself beforehand. In other words when you arrive at the waterside every float in your box should already be accurately shotted so that you can tell at a glance what is needed.

The answer is to shot all your floats accurately at home before going fishing using a bucket or the bath but, when doing so, bear in mind the additional weight which will be placed on the float, by hook, line and bait. Heavier baits, of course, will make a bigger difference. Once you have established the shotting capacity of any float to your satisfaction, mark it clearly. Some anglers do this by painting on a code of their own, using different symbols to signify different sizes of shot. Still others use the extremely useful transfers now sold in many tackle shops. The best of these are waterproof and extremely durable.

With regard to shotting patterns, I have been as specific as I could with each float and, with only one exception, the diagrams tell you all you need to know. The exception is when the wind is blowing in your face. When this happens the pattern must be altered for your problem has become one of getting your tackle out while guarding against back tangles round the float.

The answer is to put a heavier shot on down the line in the tell-tale position near the hook. For instance if, before the wind sprang up, you were using a BB in this position you would increase this with a swan at the same time subtracting the appropriate amount to retain the balance from the other shots you have further up the line.

This is particularly simple with all those floats which carry bulk shot. In this case you simply take your big shot —a swan—from the bulk cluster and add the small shot you have removed from the tell-tale to the bulk.

Always begin your angling day by plumbing the depth. This doesn't need saying to old hands but it's truly remarkable how many anglers don't carry out this vital function. If you know the depth of water and things start happening which affect the way your tackle is behaving, you usually know more clearly what is wrong and what needs changing.

Having taken all these basic precautions gear your mind then to always expect the unexpected. In the normal way it's reasonable to presume that a bite will submerge your float. Alternatively, however, your float may lift. It may quiver. It may move slowly along the surface. A very basic tip then: strike at any unnatural movement of the float. The result may not always be a fish but at least you will always have the satisfaction of knowing that if it was you would have caught it. And all it costs you is the small effort of re-casting.

Which leads me to another important tip: always inspect your bait after retrieving your tackle. For, like me, you are bound to discover that there are times when your bait has been chewed yet there has not been the slightest sign on your float to suggest this. The answer is to move the bottom shot on your line—the tell-tale—nearer the hook. If this doesn't work, and it should in most cases, try moving this shot in the opposite direction for your tackle might be needing to clear some underwater obstruction you can't see.

Remember, too, that not all the floats I have talked about are designed specifically to go under on the bite. Some will but some are most unlikely to do this. The tip here: where the body of a float is at the lower end of the stem the tendency to produce lift bites is always greater.

Lift bites are also more likely whenever the tell-tale shot is moved nearer the hook.

Casting is particularly important when float fishing. The wrong cast can make the tackle misbehave badly and cause you heartbreaking tangles which, in turn, cost valuable fishing time. The golden rule is to always cast *into* the wind and *never* with it. For instance, if the wind is blowing downstream, cast upstream. The only exception to this: when the wind is blowing from directly behind you then cast straight with it.

As a caster I invariably throw underhand. It takes some mastering, especially when you want to cast constantly and accurately to one chosen spot.

At the same time, I admit that most anglers cast overhand, particularly when fishing big waters. There is nothing wrong with this—my decision to be a permanent underhander is a personal choice—but with certain float tackles overhand casting can be fatal. The tip here: always cast underhand when the body of the float is at the bottom of the stem. A good yardstick: this is almost invariably when you are loose float fishing with the float attached to the line by the bottom ring only.

One general point I would like to make at this final stage is that while I was basically a match fisherman and while the floats I have told you about will do all you could want them to do in a match, they are equally applicable to pleasure fishing. I have the feeling—perhaps wrongly—that the average pleasure angler might feel that these floats might not be for him. He couldn't be more wrong. In fact, I am certain that if the average angler would take the trouble to become conversant with these floats and their use, his catches would treble in the first season which came after and would improve even further in the seasons which followed. And you can consider that a guarantee!

Index